T0271535

Talking with Bereaved People

by the same author

Setting Up and Facilitating Bereavement Support Groups
A Practical Guide
Dodie Graves
ISBN 978 1 84905 271 9
eISBN 978 0 85700 573 1

of related interest

The Essential Guide to Life After Bereavement
Beyond Tomorrow
Judy Carole Kauffmann and Mary Jordan
Foreword by Ciaran Devane
ISBN 978 1 84905 335 8
eISBN 978 0 85700 669 1

After the Suicide
Helping the Bereaved to Find a Path from Grief to Recovery
Kari Dyregrov, Einar Plyhn and Gudrun Dieserud
Foreword by John R. Jordan
ISBN 978 1 84905 211 5
eISBN 978 0 85700 445 1

Effective Grief and Bereavement Support
The Role of Family, Friends, Colleagues, Schools and Support Professionals
Kari Dyregrov and Atle Dyregrov
Foreword by Magne Raundalen
ISBN 978 1 84310 667 8
eISBN 978 1 84642 833 3

Writing in Bereavement
A Creative Handbook
Jane Moss
Part of the Writing for Therapy or Personal Development series
ISBN 978 1 84905 212 2
eISBN 978 0 85700 450 5

Talking About Death and Bereavement in School
How to Help Children Aged 4 to 11 to Feel Supported and Understood
Ann Chadwick
ISBN 978 1 84905 246 7
eISBN 978 0 85700 527 4

What Does Dead Mean?
A Book for Young Children to Help Explain Death and Dying
Caroline Jay and Jenni Thomas
Illustrated by Unity-Joy Dale
ISBN 978 1 84905 355 6
eISBN 978 0 85700 705 6

Talking with Bereaved People

An Approach for Structured
and Sensitive Communication

Dodie Graves

Jessica Kingsley *Publishers*
London and Philadelphia

First published in 2009
by Jessica Kingsley Publishers
116 Pentonville Road
London N1 9JB, UK
and
400 Market Street, Suite 400
Philadelphia, PA 19106, USA

www.jkp.com

Copyright © Dodie Graves 2009
Printed digitally sinec 2013

Library of Congress Cataloging in Publication Data
Graves, Dodie.
    Talking with bereaved people : an approach for structured and sensitive communication /
      Dodie Graves.
      p. cm.
    Includes bibliographical references and index.
     ISBN 978-1-84310-988-4 (pb : alk. paper) 1. Bereavement--Psychological aspects. 2. Death--Psychological aspects. I. Title.
    BF575.G7G689 2009
    155.9'37--dc22
                2009010540

British Library Cataloguing in Publication Data
A CIP catalogue record for this book is available from the British Library

ISBN 978 1 84310 988 4
eISBN 978 0 85700 162 7

Dedication

To the memory of my mother, Edna, who bravely supported us through an early bereavement; and to Robin, who lived briefly but touched many lives.

Acknowledgements

I wish to acknowledge my colleagues at Compton Hospice, and especially Jane Rowley for her support and encouragement along the way; and to Dee Elcock for her excellent technical skills and for standing in the gap during the writing period. I wish to acknowledge the team of bereavement visitors, without whom this would have been a longer time in the making, and to whom I am indebted for their commitment, support and shared experiences – this is as much their book as it is mine. To my supervisor, Lesley Whittaker who first encouraged me to even think about sharing this way of working by writing a book, many thanks for believing it would be useful to others. I wish to acknowledge the Marie Curie Hospice in Solihull, Birmingham, and the Douglas Macmillan Hospice, in Stoke on Trent, Staffordshire, for allowing us to view their guidelines on self harm and suicide. Finally, my thanks go to my husband, Charles, for reading and rereading the manuscript and giving me constructive feedback, as ever in a gentle and caring way.

Disclaimer

None of the anecdotal illustrations in this book are true to life. All illustrations are composites of real situations, and any resemblance to people living or dead is coincidental.

Contents

PREFACE   11

THE BASICS OF TALKING WITH BEREAVED PEOPLE   20

A BRIEF INTRODUCTION TO THE SIX ELEMENTS   32

Chapter 1:   Element 1: There is a story   35

Chapter 2:   Element 2: There is a relationship   64

Chapter 3:   Element 3: There is a life to celebrate   93

Chapter 4:   Element 4: There is a legacy left behind   107

Chapter 5:   Element 5: There is a strategy for coping   119

Chapter 6:   Element 6: There is a journey undertaken   146

Chapter 7:   There are difficult issues to explore   164

             Conclusion   182

APPENDIX: AN OVERVIEW OF THE SIX ELEMENTS   185

REFERENCES   189

FURTHER READING   190

USEFUL RESOURCES   192

INDEX   198

Preface

A few years ago, I was confronted with a challenge that set me thinking about what we actually do when we are talking with bereaved people. Let me share with you something of that challenge which came from a volunteer bereavement support worker.

Angie shifted uncomfortably. 'I have to tell you that I don't much like the idea of bereavement theories!' She laughed nervously.

'Oh,' I said. 'You're not keen on the idea of studying the theories.'

'No, I'm not. I've nursed all my life and sat with people and talked to them over the years as a Macmillan nurse and you just don't need theories, you need to let them talk. And these theories…what do they teach you anyway about how to be with people when they're hurting? I'm no academic and I don't want to be. No, I'm sorry I just don't hold with them, and until somebody comes up with something practical I can do, I don't want to be inundated with theories!'

I have the privilege of coordinating a bereavement service in a hospice where there is a team of extremely committed and highly motivated volunteers of all ages and from varying backgrounds who do the bulk of the bereavement support work for the hospice. They are trained listeners, experienced in the area of bereavement from their own experience, from their training and from their work with many bereaved people over the years. When I first took up this position, I came with a desire to know more about the grieving process and the bereavement theories, as I had previously worked in a more general counselling practice for many years. I felt too that the team of volunteers might also benefit from what I was learning, so I wanted to set about doing some training on the contemporary theories and models.

In my discussion with Angie, I had to concede that she had a point, and we had a profitable discussion around what she had experienced in her visiting. In a way it had resonated with something I had been working on for a while. There are theories that help us understand what bereavement can look like and how people might respond and why. However, many of the health-care staff and nurses I have trained in the past, as well as volunteers in church settings and other agencies, have asked the question, 'What do I talk about with someone who's been bereaved without doing any harm?' That seems to be part of the issue for those who are not qualified as psychologists and counsellors. How do we sensitively communicate with bereaved people so that they feel we understand? We do not want to be giving them platitudes and saying things to them to make us feel better.

There are so many things one might say when confronted with stressful situations that we could cheerfully kick ourselves for afterwards. Let me give you a few examples of what one might say and live to regret. After each one, I am giving an imaginary response that might be the thoughts of the bereaved person.

Here's a favourite, especially at funerals: 'Well, she lived a long life, that's something to be grateful for.'

'No, it isn't. She lived a long life and was always a part of my life; she was always there when I needed her. What am I going to do without her? I've never known life without her.'

Another might be, 'He's out of pain now at least. You wouldn't have wanted him to suffer, would you?'

'No, I wouldn't have wanted that, but I want him back and it just makes me feel worse – guilty for feeling like this when you say those kinds of things.'

And after a sudden death: 'At least she didn't have to suffer a long, slow death. She went quickly and that's better for her.'

'It might have been better for her, but I feel terrible. We're all in shock, and I can't think how it can be better. It's just terrible and you don't know what you're saying. You just don't understand.'

After a suicide: 'The poor thing, she must have been in a terrible state and feeling so alone to do something so awful. What a tragic waste of life. You must feel terrible.'

'Yes, I do, and now I feel worse because you've made it sound as if nobody cared and especially me, her mother. How could I have known she was going to do something like this? She gave us no warning. You don't know how it's been for the past few months, walking around on egg shells with her. You just don't understand.'

In a nutshell, words like these, though well meaning, can be very wounding and insensitive. Generally, people are usually too polite to respond the way they really feel and might just agree with you. People are often strange and awkward, perhaps embarrassed around those who are bereaved; people tell me that neighbours will walk on the other side of the road or go back in the house rather than have to speak. We simply don't know what to say. But most people would want you to say something, and sometimes the fewer words the better. Perhaps: 'I'm so sorry. I can't imagine how you must be feeling.' Or, 'This must be such a difficult time for you.' Or, 'This is so sad. I don't know what to say.' Just about anything will feel right if it comes from your own genuine struggle with the awfulness of death and loss, and you just want to convey something of that struggle. You can enter into their situation, as long as the emphasis is not on you; as long as you do not turn the topic to your own experiences. So many people talk about their own situation with a newly bereaved person, giving a blow by blow account of what happened in their own circumstances. It does not feel good to be on the receiving end of that. No matter how interesting it might be, it is not useful or comforting for the person who is suffering their own loss to know what happened to you.

As I was beginning to write the manuscript for this book, my mother died. She had suffered from dementia for a long time which had robbed us of her for a number of years before her death. My sisters and I went through the dying vigil in the nursing home and we experienced a strange detachment from the outside world as we watched and waited with her. Those involved in the nursing and care of my mother were intimately acquainted with every hour. But when we came away from the death scene, the world outside was going on just the same and others we met had no idea of what we had been through. Friends and colleagues were limited in what they could say. They had not known my mother and I did not have time to explain it all to them either. What is more, I did not have the emotional energy to tell them. They would not have been able to enter my story without sitting and listening, taking the time to hear that story and explore with me what it meant for me to experience the pain of death and the loss of my mother. I heard some of the things I have just described. Mostly people just said things like, 'We're here for you if you need us.' It was very nice to hear that but there were only a few who came and said, 'I've just come to see how you're doing.' How inviting that was to me to give voice to what I might have been feeling or thinking at the time.

As my experience proved, even professionals might find themselves slipping into platitudes or avoiding getting into the details of the way someone is feeling. If you are a friend, or a volunteer who visits bereaved people, or a professional person who counsels, you might want to know what to talk about with bereaved people in a sensitive way that helps them and brings them some measure of comfort, knowing that you understand. Whether you only have a brief time with someone or the privilege of more time over a longer period, there are some things you can talk about that can benefit a bereaved person and be significant for them.

Not all bereaved people will need counselling or support. However, I do think it is important to have a framework for thinking about what you talk about, and to have some questions that might be of help at the time when you are in conversation with those who have been bereaved. In this book, I will be describing a framework you might use for a conversation, or several conversations, with bereaved people. For those of you who might be interested in how I came to this framework, here is a brief history of how I came to put it together.

I had attended a workshop where Robert Neimeyer, an American psychologist, led us in a fascinating review of his model on bereavement work coming from a Meaning Reconstruction point of view (rebuilding meaning in the life of a client after a death). I had been stimulated to turn my thoughts again to the question of how to support bereaved people in a practical way. What had I observed us doing, myself and the bereavement support workers? I came to some insights, based on some of the theories I had read and the experiences in coming alongside bereaved people. What do we listen to? What does the bereaved person tell us? I needed to let the bereaved people I had listened to over the years inform me.

What I had observed is that a bereaved person often wants to tell you their story, the details of what happened, usually beginning with the story of the death and other stories of the illness or events leading up to the death. Then along with the story they start to talk about the person who died and their story together. They will often talk about their relationship and the relationship that others had with their loved one. The writings and research of Tony Walter, a British sociologist, have been very helpful in providing insight into this area.

Someone who is bereaved may also be struggling to come to terms with the meaning behind the life and death of their loved one. What was it all about? 'He was a good man. So many people came to the funeral; I didn't realize he knew so many people.' What I learnt from Robert Neimeyer was that there can be opportunities at some point in a conversation with a bereaved person to celebrate the life of the deceased, and to explore what they have left behind. A point when you can help them to think about the deceased's legacy to the world, to their family and to their friends. This can help create some meaning out of the void that death leaves. They also have to make huge adjustments in their lives, having to view themselves and the rest of their lives in a different way. An American philosopher, Thomas Attig, has written work that is helpful in thinking about the way bereaved people need to 'relearn' their worlds.

People seem to approach their bereavement in a variety of ways, and everyone grieves uniquely, but there exist some familiar themes and patterns. The work of Terry Martin and Kenneth Doka has been helpful, based on the idea that there are different patterns of grieving. These might or might not be related to male or female gender characteristics, but might be more about a style of relating to the world, or a strategy for coping that the person has built up or that is innate to them.

Perhaps most of all, the most profound understanding I have gained, from my own life experiences and listening to others, is that people are on a journey, and the grief journey is a real one. The works of other psychologists who work in bereavement, Colin Murray Parkes from the palliative care world of hospices, and the American psychologist William Worden, continue to be helpful in recognizing the kind of phases or tasks that are 'sign posts' along the way on this journey.

Story – relationship – celebrating a life – legacies left behind – strategies for coping – the journey of grief – these six elements were the things people were talking about. What I have done with these areas is to put them into a structure that would be useful for anyone engaging in conversation with someone who is bereaved. I have, for ease of description, identified these six elements of a bereavement conversation, and they form the foundation of this book.

WHAT YOU WILL FIND IN THE BOOK

At this point, I will say a little about what you can expect to find in the book, the scope of it, as well as the terminology I am using and the rationale behind it. In each chapter I discuss one of the six elements and what commonly accompanies it from the perspective of the bereaved person. In each chapter, I also identify a listening activity that you might find useful. In Chapter 1 I also give brief consideration to some of the basic listening skills, giving some ideas about basic concepts in this important skill area.

In each chapter I also provide some suggestions for appropriate lines of conversation that you could use at various places in your dialogue, and list some questions to ask. For those who are quite bold and are involved in carrying out creative work with people, I have identified some techniques you might find helpful and have given some simple directions on using these techniques. You do not need to be trained in counselling before using the advice contained within this book, but you do need to ensure that you listen carefully.

I would also strongly recommend that you try these activities out for yourself before you do them with a bereaved person. You can do this within your organization or with a trusted friend. This is not to say that you have to do all of these activities, or indeed any of them. They are there to be used discreetly and always for a purpose. Sometimes you may wish to focus the person who talks about all sorts of things except the person who died, or the person who can not stay with one subject. Sometimes you may wish to touch on something that has not been expressed in words. Sometimes you may wish to help the person organize their thoughts and memories so that they can see the wood for the trees.

You will also find in each chapter a brief discussion about what you might experience as a listener when faced with the bereaved person's experiences. I raise some common issues that arise, and direct you to useful further reading.

Because I hope you will interact with this material, at times I ask you to think reflectively through some of the issues. It can be helpful to spend time putting your thoughts down on paper before you proceed with reading. Finally, the Appendix contains a table showing an overview of the six elements, which incorporates summaries of appropriate activities, questions, techniques and associated theory. You can use it as a quick reference. I have limited the scope of this book to exploring what you might talk about (and, to an extent, how to talk) with a bereaved adult, and particularly how you might support them in coming to terms with, and processing the death of someone they have loved. It is not my intention to address how to work with bereaved children or with people with learning disabilities, though I think this is an approach that would be helpful with both groups of people, using more creative activities to help explore the dimensions.

About the terms and words I have used: for the sake of brevity and ease, I refer to the bereaved person as 'the client'. I have also referred to the person who is doing the bereavement support as the 'support worker' so as to simplify the matter. You might be reading this as a counsellor, or a health worker or a member of a pastoral team; I have used the term 'support worker' for simplicity and consistency. I think the term 'support worker' describes what we do best when we are talking with bereaved people, regardless of whether we are doing it as a professional, as a volunteer, or as a friend. What we are doing is working to support them by listening. I have also chosen to use the word 'session' rather than 'visit' as some people might be seen in an agency's rooms rather than having a visit at home, and again this is only for simplicity and consistency.

What I hope you will find in this book is an approach for non academics like Angie and me. You will note, however, that I have included some of the ideas of those whose work is in the academic realm. I have done this in order to illustrate where I have found the work of theorists helpful in clarifying and supporting what I am proposing. This approach, then, is for those of you who come into contact with bereaved people and want to know what to talk about and how to be of some support through the dark days of pain, anguish, lethargy or manic activity that might surround the grieving person. I offer this approach to the world of bereavement workers in organizations such as hospices, palliative care units and other bereavement care agencies, to workers in church pastoral teams, social workers and other professional health workers. It is for anyone who comes into contact with bereaved people and has time for meaningful conversation.

I field tested this approach with the team of volunteer bereavement support workers during their training and supervision sessions. We discussed each element and they have provided me with contributions from their many years of experience. What you will see in the chapters about each element are some of the results of our discussions in these training sessions. We found that it did not matter if we were meeting with those of different cultures to ours, or those of different religious faiths or those with none; the approach takes into account where the client is and their own cultural and religious contexts.

What has been the bereavement team's response to this approach?

Barbara said, 'I always look at the overview of the six elements (see page 32–33) before I go out to a visit and see where we are and possibly where we might go in the next appointment. And I've even begun to try some of the techniques in the tool box.'

Heather, who is very experienced in group work, gave this observation: 'I can't believe it; the very next day after our training (looking at celebrating the life and the legacies left behind) we were doing just that in the group. I felt very able to explore it all further with them because we'd talked about it and thought about the type of questions to ask and how to validate what they were saying.'

Mike, usually a bit sceptical about things until he's tried them out, liked the underpinning theory and the structure which felt quite natural to him.

Finally, I will let Angie speak. She was thoroughly delighted. 'Now you're talking my language. I can see myself in this approach. I do this, so I'm happy. If you want to put in the theories for good measure, that's up to you. But this is what I can use. This is practical.' At least as far as Angie was concerned, I had come up to the challenge.

I sincerely hope you will find something here to help you think through your conversations with the bereaved people you encounter. I know that I may not be addressing all your questions and thoughts on the subject of bereavement, but I have limited the scope of this work to looking at how we can talk with bereaved people in sensitive ways, in order for them to feel supported.

The basics of talking with bereaved people

How do you talk to someone who has been bereaved and what do you say that can be meaningful? There is much said to bereaved people that can be categorized, at best as platitudes, and at worst as unhelpful. What you want to do is join the hurting person in their struggle without being superficial, patronizing or offering unsolicited advice. Unfortunately, a good deal of what people say comes out of the way they think about death, grief and bereavement. Every one of us will have some opinions or understandings about grief and bereavement learned from personal experience or passed down to us in 'folk lore' fashion, or through some training we have undertaken previously. In this chapter, I will first address some of the basic philosophies about grief and bereavement by explaining what kind of thinking goes on when I am talking to bereaved people using the six elements. Second, I will address a number of basic practicalities that would be helpful to think about before you start to talk with bereaved people.

BASIC PHILOSOPHIES

Ruth, one of a group of newly trained volunteers, told me at her sixth month review, 'Well, you see, Dodie, it's like this; I leave all my prejudices and concerns at the door and concentrate only on the person and their story.' I'm sure Ruth thought she was saying the right thing and believing that this was possible and in fact true for her. But I had to explain to her, gently I hope, to help her see that she takes all of herself into a meeting with her clients, her prejudices, her concerns as well as her understandings about life, death and bereavement. Sometimes this might mean being affected by what the bereaved person says because it touches into something we have experienced ourselves. Sometimes we might disagree in our heart and mind with what is being said or done. Understanding what is going on for us is one of the keys to good working with bereaved people.

We can be affected by people's stories and their pain, and our ways of responding might be influenced by the things we have understood to be true over the years. It is especially important that we tease out our own understandings and our beliefs about grief and bereavement. Many of those understandings have to be redefined, as they have come to us via our parents, via others we have listened to and taken note of and via society's collective thinking. The sort of thing I am referring to is the notion that people must 'let go and move on'; another is that it is wrong if people make 'shrines' to their loved ones; and then there is the belief that if they are still grieving after a year, there is something wrong. We may need to reassess some of our thinking in the light of what research informs us about people's actual experiences. We have to be careful about how we approach people and how we 'direct' people who are vulnerable.

One of the most important underpinning philosophies is to not talk with our clients about 'letting go' of their loved one. So many people think it is necessary to let the loved one go before they can successfully start to live again. But the surviving relatives are still attached to the ones they love, as we will see in Chapter 2 when we examine this concept further. So, what would 'letting go' mean to the bereaved person? In their understanding, they would have to leave their loved one behind. Even Freud, who had been an advocate for detachment from, and letting go of, the object of affection, found reality different to theory. In his great sorrow after the death of his beloved daughter in child birth and the subsequent death of her son at four years of age, he could not contemplate letting go of his love for them. Nine years later he wrote to a friend whose son had died:

> No matter what may fill the gap, even if it be filled completely, it nevertheless remains something else. And actually this is how it should be. It is the only way of perpetuating that love which we do not want to relinquish. (Klass, Silverman and Nickman 1996, p.6)

So, if we are not talking about letting go, what do we understand about the place of the deceased in the life of the bereaved person? One may understand that there will always be a loss, and that life will never be the same again without the loved one. It will be different; the place that was once occupied by that loved one is now empty. One may understand that, in time, a new place can be found for that person in the affections, memories and daily life of the bereaved person. In time the pain is not as intense and raw as it once was. The loss will not always be at the fore-front of the bereaved person's life; rather the loved one is still loved, but can be sited in another place. William Worden has identified four tasks of mourning, the fourth of which is to relocate the deceased in a differ-ent emotional place. This task to be accomplished by the bereaved person is so that they may 'find an appropriate place for the dead in their emotional lives – a place that will enable them to go on living effectively in the world' (Worden 1991, p.17).

We also do not talk about the client 'moving on' which is a concept that so easily rolls off the tongue when people are talking about the bereaved. 'I told her she just needed to get on with her life and move on now. It's been six months since he died.' Even some professionals who work in palliative care can operate with this concept underpinning their assessments. 'He's not doing so well, he's got stuck in his grief and isn't able to move on. Can you see him?' In the mind of the bereaved person this concept of 'moving on' may have negative connotations. They can think, 'Moving on in my life means I'll have to let go of my loved one, and leave them behind, and I don't want to.' These concepts are often hard for the bereaved person as they want to continue the memory of the deceased and not forget them, or leave them behind.

If we do not talk about moving on, then what do we talk about? One may talk about living with the pain while coping in different ways. There is an adjustment to be made. I use this analogy: being bereaved can in some ways be likened to being an amputee. If you had your leg amputated you would feel the pain for quite a long time. Amputees often say they think they have still got the limb that was amputated, and if they were to try to walk they would be convinced they could put their weight on the missing limb. However, they would soon fall over. A crutch is needed until a prosthetic limb is supplied. This is how one may think of bereavement. Being wounded means needing to be healed and going through a healing process takes time, experiencing considerable pain and discomfort along the way. Metaphorically speaking, the bereaved person may think that when they get up to walk by themselves they will fall over. Sometimes they feel their loved one is still there; if only they could reach out and touch them it would be all right and they would be whole again.

Another underpinning philosophy essential to our work is that we are not 'the experts' with the answers about how people respond. So many people who are bereaved want to know if they are 'doing it' right. They are also often afraid that if they are suppressing something now, it will come back and debilitate them or paralyse them in some way later on. So they look to us, the professionals, and they want to have our 'expert opinion'. The fantasy might be that they want a 'fix' – 'a course of treatment' for this pain. Sadly, we are not able to fix this pain; no pill can ever take this kind of pain away. In reality, we tell people they might initially feel worse after seeing us, as during the time we have spent together memories and emotions have been stirred up.

If we are not the experts with answers, then what can we offer to bereaved people who are hurting? I believe sincerely that we offer some people, perhaps most, a time to talk about their loved one: a time to think, to feel, to cry, and to process what is going on for them. It is an opportunity for some to talk to someone who is not part of the grieving family, who will not be offended by what is said, and will not tell them they should be 'over this now', or they should be getting on with life. We are outsiders who are not part of their daily struggle, and at best we might be able to help them think through how they will make adjustments to their new circumstances. At worst we will have listened well to them as they have told their stories and as they have remembered their loved ones. We are not experts in their life, we go tentatively, learning about them as we go, and offering our observations to them very carefully.

We also do not get drawn in to giving advice about how to handle their grief. Advice giving is one of the most common pitfalls for anyone wanting to support bereaved people. When I interview prospective volunteers for the role of support worker, I ask what it is that makes them think they can be supportive of bereaved people. Some of them say to me, 'I think I can help because lots of my friends and people at work come to me for advice.' This is not what I'm looking for. Advice is easy to give.

> 'If I were you, I would…' 'Have you tried…?' 'Have you thought of…?' 'Why don't you…?' 'My suggestion would be that you…'

It can make us feel good to offer advice, it is practical and it is something that perhaps makes us feel significant. In reality, it is not helpful to the person who just needs you to listen.

In my counselling training days, I well recall one of our lecturers stressing that we could prepare ourselves for starting off in our careers as counsellors by reading good detective novels, and resist going to the end of the book to find out who did it! What he was telling us was that we needed to be like good sleuths, not taking things for granted and not assuming things. So, another important underpinning philosophy is to be 'seekers not tellers'. Try to be curious in a sensitive way, not taking for granted that we understand what is being felt or said. Try not to make assumptions about what they are saying, and not to think we understand what they mean when they say things like, 'It's worse at night.' We need to find out what makes it worse. What do they think about and feel? Do they mean when they go to bed and try to sleep? Do they mean they are having dreams or nightmares? One might assume they are saying they are lonelier at night with no one there. If we operate on that assumption and just nod and appear sympathetic instead of investigating what they mean, we might miss out on a lot of information and the opportunity to support them through a difficult time. So it might be better to say, 'You're struggling at night, then.' It is hoped this will encourage them to tell you more and then you can ask, 'What do you find particularly difficult?'

Perhaps one of the most important philosophies is that, in listening carefully to the client's stories, we actively explore the client's present struggles and their future concerns. We need to enable them to assess how their assumptions, their values, their belief systems, their life style patterns have either failed them or sustained them in the way they are adjusting, or not adjusting, to their changed life situation. We need to help them examine where they have been forced to re-evaluate their values and beliefs and hence their lifestyle. Throughout the listening process, we need to be able to identify with the client where they are struggling with adjustments to this new life.

BASIC PRACTICALITIES

I think just a few things need to be said around some basic practicalities of listening to people. These suggestions come out of my own practice and experience and if you differ from me, that is fine, but I would ask you to think through some of the issues that are raised here and perhaps you might wish to initiate some discussions with your peer support workers or professional colleagues. I will also give brief consideration to setting up your support session, getting someone to support you, and looking after yourself.

Titles

As I get older I am beginning to appreciate what an elderly relative talked about when she told us that she was fed up of being called 'Evie' by all and sundry on her hospital visits. She wanted to be known by her surname Mrs... She said she felt it was more professional. After all, she didn't consider them to be her friends, and only her family and friends called her by her first name. We do not know what people want to be known as until we ask them. Initially on the phone or at a first meeting face to face, I will address someone as Mr or Mrs or Miss ... then I will introduce myself: 'I'm happy for you to call me Dodie if you would like to. How would you like me to address you? By your surname or your first name?' It sounds old fashioned, outdated even, but it works really well. People can be free to say, 'I'm happy for you to call me...' Or, 'I actually like being called Miss...' People will not feel they have a right to be addressed as they wish to be if you have already begun calling them by their first name. So, we want to try to respect people by allowing them to tell us what their preference is in this small but significant area.

Time

It is important at the outset, when you are establishing what and who you are, to talk about how much time you have. If you are in someone else's house, this is especially the case as the boundaries of an official 'quiet room' are not in place. If you do not establish the time boundary, they will assume you have an indefinite amount of time and may be offended when you tell them it is time to leave. If I can not see a convenient clock, I tell them: 'I'll take my watch off and put it so that I can see it, and I hope you won't be offended if I occasionally look at it.' No one seems to have been offended so far, because they were forewarned. But make sure you do warn them otherwise they will say, 'She was very nice but she spent most of the time looking at her watch.'

Tears

What do we do when someone starts to cry, sometimes uncontrollably? Maybe this touches into some of our own issues and long held practices. What not to say is, 'Don't cry now, it'll only make you feel worse.' Neither should we say, 'I'm so sorry I've upset you.' Nor do we offer to make a cup of tea or coffee in the face of tears. This is a very distracting thing to do – it gets us nicely out of the way when things get 'hot' or embarrassing, especially in a hospital or hospice setting (perhaps we hope they'll be over it by the time the kettle's boiled!). This leaves the client alone at their most vulnerable time. Also do not reach out to touch the client (more of this below). This seems heartless to some people, but our silence and our gentle presence is more of a help at a time when someone is upset. Make sure they have a tissue if they need it. We have learnt to take out little packets of tissues with us when we go to people's homes so we are ready to offer the packet when someone is crying. Some schools of thought would not do even that, but we would rather the person have the tissue if they need it than get up to go searching for one, which of course removes them for a time from their emotions.

What one can do, then, is wait for them to settle themselves, and gently say, if it is needed: 'You're feeling quite emotional at this point. What's going on for you right now?'

What is really important is that you acknowledge their tears and the fact that they are upset. They need to know you have noticed. Some people will feel embarrassed crying in front of you, especially the first time it happens, so you might also say: 'I wonder if you're feeling embarrassed at crying in front of me?'

Even if they are not, it will feel good to them that you have even thought to ask them. Try not to fill the silence when people are upset; let them gather themselves. It might feel like a long time to you, but it won't to them as they try to bring their tears under control.

Touch

Another thing some of us have had to struggle with, as part of our natural way of responding, is that we do not get up and give the client a hug or put an arm around their shoulder when they are upset. Think about how you would feel if a stranger gave you a hug. I personally would hate to be hugged when I am crying – I want to wipe my nose and get a grip of myself, and I do not want to be smothered in a stranger's chest, however well meaning that person might be. I want to be allowed to feel my emotions, and then start to make sense of them. I am not sure how others feel, but one can not assume that touch is right for everyone, especially given that some people might have experienced some difficult situations involving touch in the past. We also do not know how our touch or hug is going to be interpreted and it changes the relationship. If you are reading this as a friend of someone who has been bereaved, then you will know what your relationship can take, and if a hug is the right thing, then obviously that may be the appropriate thing to do. In the main, though, for those of us who work in the area of psychosocial and emotional support, my advice is that it is better to err on the side of caution. Clients will hear our concern, they will feel our compassion, and they will appreciate the appropriateness of our verbal connection rather than our physical contact with them.

You might ask me, 'What do I do if the client hugs me at the end as I'm going out through the door?' My answer is to receive it but not to return it. In other words, you do not show you are willing to accept the change in the relationship. I will often pre-empt something like this by holding out my hand to shake theirs as a way of connecting; it is warm and friendly while remaining professional. Clients soon learn that you are in a certain role, and while you are listening to some of the most difficult emotional and personal parts of their lives, you are not there as a friend – unless you are, of course!

Setting up a working agreement or 'contracting'

At the outset it will be important to establish what kind of support you can offer to the bereaved person. If you are not a qualified counsellor, be specific about the type of support you can offer:

> 'I'm not a counsellor; I'm a trained support worker with experience in the area of bereavement. If either, or both of us, feels you need the support of a qualified counsellor, I will support you in getting that help. It might be, for example, that there are issues you're facing that need the expertise of a counsellor.'

If you are a health worker, you can say much the same thing, identifying your professional role. In some settings a professional may be giving treatment, e.g. physiotherapy or complementary therapy, where a conversation arises quite naturally out of the type of therapy being given. If this happens to you, you can establish what kind of support to continue with and may want to refer the patient. If you are a friend you will be able to advise your friend to seek further support if you think there are things that need looking into that are out of your depth.

When you are setting up the appointment at the client's home, also make sure that the person you are visiting knows that you are expecting to see them on their own, so that you do not get surprised by the whole family turning up to see you. Some people will have a member of the family come in or be there just to check you out, and they will leave when they feel you are safe. We are quite clear about seeing someone alone as this is part of the agreement I make with the client on the phone when establishing the first contact in my role as coordinator.

Confidentiality is a very important aspect of this work. It is very important in any field of work with people, but there are limits, and the client needs to know you will be sharing with someone who is qualified to hear. In other words, you need to assure them you will not be sharing what they have told you in the local neighbourhood, the church, or with members of your family when you get home, or with your colleagues at work. It is important to let the bereaved person know that you do have a supervisor who supports you in this type of work and you will be taking the details of your conversations to that person so that they support you both. What they tell you will be shared in a professional setting in the bereavement team under supervision, which is ethically correct for this type of work.

It is vital at the initial session to be clear about what you would do if you feel they are at risk of doing any harm to themselves or anyone else. In our organization we are agreed that in the instance of a threatened suicide, the support workers would need to break that confidentiality by speaking to the supervisor or perhaps the client's doctor in certain instances. I have written briefly in Chapter 7 on what you might do in the event of people talking about suicidal thoughts.

Supervision

When we listen to people's stories and experience their grief it is always impacting. If you are part of an organization that offers bereavement care, make sure they support you in offering you supervision by a qualified and/or experienced person. There are several important issues to look at here:

1. It will be necessary to trust your supervisor with things that impact you, without being, or feeling, judged for your responses.

2. It is important you can explore even the negative responses towards a bereaved person with someone who will understand and help you.

3. It is important for you to be able to talk to another person in a legitimate and confidential place. As the bereavement support workers often say to me, 'I've really needed to get rid of that as I can't talk to anyone else about it.'

Just a word here to those who might belong to a church group. The vicar or minister of your church may not be the most appropriate person to supervise you, as they are not necessarily trained supervisors. They may also be known to or by the bereaved person, and will have a different role to yours in that person's life. Maybe they have to buy in the services of a supervisor for you. In the following chapters, I will be indicating the type of things you might need to take to supervision and explore, so that your support work with people is enhanced by becoming more self aware.

Looking after yourself

There are considerable rewards for us as we support those who have been bereaved; the sense of having supported others and being of use can be part of our own self-esteem building. It can be a life enriching and enhancing experience, a real privilege to be entrusted with the stories of people's lives and deaths. However, it can take its toll. Be aware of your own needs. One of our bereavement support workers lives alone and shared with us in supervision that she felt very low after sessions with a client in the evening and found it difficult to settle afterwards. She came to a decision that for her personally, and given her life circumstances, she would not book appointments in the evening or at weekends. She needed to look after herself too. It might be a good idea not to put sessions with bereaved people into a busy day, as you might not have the energy you need for your own activities afterwards. Being busy before you see someone who is bereaved is also not an ideal thing to do, as you will need to settle into the listening mode without too many internal distractions going on for you.

We need to be aware of our own life changes. When serious life events happen to us, we will need to take time out from supporting others. When my mother died, I was not able to take on bereavement work as I normally do. I had to give myself some space from that close connection with other bereaved people. It is not only our own bereavement issues; it can be many other things that happen to distract us. So be aware that as a support worker you need to be sure of your own support networks and of your own limitations. We can be tired after listening to others' grief stories. Another of our bereavement team says she always goes to a certain café and sits with her note book to write her notes, so that she puts down her thoughts and then is able to move on into the rest of her day.

A word about note taking – ensure you understand what is required of you by your organization. We keep brief notes of the 'content' only of the session which are filed away once we have finished with the client. Our own 'process' notes (usually about the way the client was and the things that were said) that will have more details are shredded after the sessions have come to an end.

In summary, then, there are basic philosophies that underpin a conversation with a bereaved person and guide our approach to their grieving process. First, there will always be a loss; life will not be the same again; the empty space may not be filled but a new place can be found for the loved one. Second, people live with the pain of loss while learning to cope in different ways, making necessary adjustments. Third, we offer bereaved people time to talk about their loved one, helping them to think about how they will make adjustments to their changed circumstances. Fourth, we are 'seekers not tellers' and, rather than offering advice, we find out what is going on for them and help them think about how they will choose to react or respond to various new situations.

There are also basic practicalities to consider before you start talking with bereaved people: addressing people without offending them; setting up the time you have available; coping with tears and handling the sensitive issue about touch. Before you start your conversation with a bereaved person you will need to establish what kind of support you are going to offer and be clear about the boundaries around it, including what to say about such things as confidentiality and supervision. Setting up with a good supervisor and looking after yourself are also important issues to consider as you think about supporting people who are going to talk in depth to you about their pains and sorrows.

In the following chapter I will briefly introduce the six elements that I have used in this approach.

A brief introduction to the six elements

'I don't want to say anything that will cause any further hurt. They're hurting enough. What can I talk about that won't do any damage?' This is a commonly stated fear among volunteers and professionals whom I meet when I am training on working with loss and grief. It is natural to feel concerned that you do not make a situation worse by saying something insensitive. But maybe these sentiments, though well meaning, are focused in the wrong place. The focus in this fear is on what the support worker can say and do, but perhaps we need to think more about what is going on for the bereaved person, than what we might be able to say.

Let me try to reassure you – in using this approach you will accompany the bereaved person on their journey so they will talk about what matters to them, and you will have a framework for guiding them when necessary. You will have six elements as a framework to help you think through what the bereaved person is talking about, and having a framework for your conversation is a way of keeping you both on track. If you are really listening to them, and you are not trying to give advice and 'expert' suggestions, then you will generally avoid doing any damage and you might help someone feel supported.

THE SIX ELEMENTS

Briefly, the six elements in the conversation with a bereaved person are as follows:

1. The story, for example, of the deceased's life, their illness, their death.

2. The relationship the deceased had with the bereaved person and with the rest of their family and friends.

3. Celebrating the life of the deceased, their achievements, their way of living and being.

4. The legacy they have left behind which is about the significant impact the deceased had on others' lives and how their character and person will be remembered.

5. The strategy for coping that the bereaved person is using to manage their loss.

6. The journey they are on as they make their way through unknown territory.

In the following chapters you will read about each element in turn, along with some suggestions of how to use them with the bereaved people you talk to. One thing I should make clear is that this model is not meant to be the definitive answer to bereavement work; it is offered as an approach that can be useful for you to use. There are many excellent theories and there are many helpful ways of working with bereaved people. This approach is only one but it is one that I have found very effective.

The six elements do not need to be followed strictly in the order given in this book, though my colleagues and I have found that it works and it is an order that feels like a natural progression. When a client does not know where to begin, you can help them start to converse in a way that will feel natural to them, but it should not be used as an inflexible, prescriptive approach. For instance, a person may begin by telling you how they are not coping, they want to know how to cope better, and they want some advice from you. According to our framework above, this would be step 5. I would listen and work with this, but it is really hard to support someone without knowing some of the details about the story of the deceased person's life, death and the relationships they had with the significant people in their lives. So, I would guide them back to elements one and two, story and relationship.

If you come to this work from a background of brief therapy, you might be used to thinking in terms of a set number of sessions. Because there are six elements it might suggest to you that each element could form the subject matter for the whole of one session. This is not how we have found the approach works in practice, as you might find that the bereaved person touches on more than one of the elements in each conversation: the conversation needs to take as much time as is needed. Because of this, I have not indicated any set time frames: sometimes, you may move through all six elements in one session. Other times, you may talk about story and relationship for a long time before moving on.

CHAPTER 1

Element 1: There is a story

✿ **There is a story**

✿ There is a relationship

✿ There is a life to celebrate

✿ There is a legacy left behind

✿ There is a strategy for coping

✿ There is a journey undertaken

As children we may have grown to love stories and adventures, especially as delaying tactics for bedtime curfews. Inherently we seem to be interested in our own stories and, as we get older, the stories of others in our own families. I expect that in a lot of families these days there will be someone tracing back the family line, interested in discovering the family skeletons, scandals or successes. It has been especially popularized by the television programmes we see on getting back to our roots and finding out about our ancestors. Everyone has a story to tell. This is true also, of course, of every bereaved person. There are many stories to be told if someone has the time and patience to listen.

The importance of story telling has been acknowledged by many who work in the area of bereavement. There are those who think that there may, or may not, be a need for everyone who is bereaved to assimilate the deceased person into their ongoing lives, but that if they did, then the best way for them to do this would be to talk with others who knew the deceased. Tony Walter (1996) is one of those who believe this to be so. Rather than coming from a psychological perspective,

Walter comes from the sociological discipline, and has used some of his own experiences as well as his research in his writings and his biographical model. He found that people wanted to talk about their loved ones, and especially wanted to talk to those who knew them in different situations. They gathered information about their loved ones, and they built a story that fitted the deceased into their own lives. This story became a lasting memorial to the deceased, and they then were able to carry on their lives with the deceased's memory in a secure place. The picture of the deceased may need to be reasonably accurate to be of any benefit, but what is more important is that it is shared – though Walter is also aware, as we are, that some circumstances of the story about the deceased might need to be kept private, and the bereaved person might want to do that. He acknowledges that we do have some difficulties in our modern and mobile society in being able to fulfil this story gathering. One, those who knew the deceased may not be easily contactable because of geographical distances; two, people who may have known the deceased at work are also not able to share easily with bereaved relatives because we live in a society where work and home are separated; and three, it is also the case that when some people have outlived their peers, there are no witnesses left to their lives who can share with those left behind.

I generally agree with what Walter is proposing, and encourage clients to find out from others about their loved ones. He does, however, think that rather than expressing emotions people benefit from the process of building the story of their loved ones by talking about the deceased. In my experience, I have understood that bereaved people can often benefit just as much from telling stories about their loved ones with someone who has not known the deceased. They can gather their fuller pictures and deeper insights from those who did know the deceased, and they can have the opportunity of talking about what they have learnt with someone who is not going to contradict them but allows them to integrate that information in whatever way they choose.

That the story, and the process of telling it, has significance in and of itself has only recently been recognized in the counselling world. Narrative Therapy acknowledges the power of and meaning to the client's story. The work of the therapist is to help the client rethink the characters in their story and their behaviours, to re-interpret their story, and explore how they might write their future stories. I have found it refreshing and encouraging reading some of the theorists who use narrative in their work with bereaved people as I feel it values the place of story telling as well as the story teller and the listener.

One of those theorists is Bronna D. Romanoff who writes as a psychotherapist, a bereavement counsellor, and a bereaved parent. She comes from a tradition of Meaning Reconstruction Therapy which recognizes that people gain meaning from their past stories that influence their thinking for their present and their future. She suggests that when telling and retelling the stories around loss, the healing takes place by 'working on' and 'working through' the loss to a point where the bereaved person feels they recognize for themselves a change in their own identity. In her work she acknowledges the value of narrative therapies (2001, p.249):

> Narrative approaches view the therapeutic process as a facilitated journey wherein the telling and mutual understanding of the client's story will enable a new coconstructed story to emerge. Although the outcome or the goal of therapy is not known at the outset, the desire and expectation of change is an explicit part of the therapeutic contract. Narrative is the vehicle for change.

She also writes about the role of the therapist which becomes not that of expert or diagnostician or even that of a healer, but 'the therapist is a listener, a witness, a companion on the journey' (p.247). Although you may not be a therapist, you can take encouragement from this view of using story and narrative, and your role as a companion to your client on their journey in your bereavement conversations. As support workers we can acknowledge and utilize the importance of our client's story, and not rush over it as if it were not part of the 'real work'. Clients often want to tell their story over and over to make some meaning of it. In a sense, it can be said that encouraging them to tell their story is indeed an important part of the 'real work' of bereavement support.

Another psychologist who works with narrative is Robert A. Neimeyer. His work has had considerable influence on how I view the importance of story in the bereavement conversation. He suggests that in reconstructing meaning after a loss it is our natural desire, as human beings, to create a 'plausible account' of those events in our lives that have been significant (2001). There is nothing in our lives that is more significant than death itself. When we work with a bereaved client we want to work with their stories in such a way as to help them gain a new perspective, to view the bigger picture and construct a 'plausible account'. He writes of the loss of a loved one in this way (2001, p.263):

> Like a novel that loses a central character in the middle chapters, the life story disrupted by loss must be reorganized, rewritten, to find a new strand of continuity that bridges the past with the future in an intelligible fashion.

I think this picture of the 'novel that loses a central character in the middle chapters' is essential for us to remember as we listen to the client's story and consider the part the deceased played in the client's life.

It might be beneficial for you to pause here and to think (with pen and paper perhaps) about the experiences you have had with bereaved people telling their stories. When you see a client (a patient's relative, or someone who has been bereaved) what is the first story they often want to tell you? How many stories do you think there might be for a client to tell? Would you be able to give a title to each story?

We are going to look now at the content of some of those stories, and think about how we can assist people in telling them so that they discover insights, meaning and a bigger picture. A story has to begin somewhere, so what is the first story that introduces the life events of this client and the one who died?

THE FIRST STORY

Without being prescriptive, I would like to offer some guidelines in describing what is true for many clients. I often find the first story to be told is about the illness of the patient or the events leading up to the death. This will be given in varying degrees of detail. During the illness, some people have written it down in their diaries as they went through every doctor's visit or hospital appointment with their loved ones. Whether they have recorded it on paper or not, the story is often memorized and it plays over and over again in their minds. Encouraging them to tell you about it is a good way of starting the conversation:

'If it's all right with you, could you tell me what happened during his illness?' Or,

'I don't know very much at all about what happened to you and… (name). I wonder if you'd mind telling me about it. It might be a suitable place to start.'

So, they might tell us about the first diagnosis, the mistakes made by medical staff, or themselves. They might speak about their guilt of not being able to do enough, or not realizing the situation was as bad as it really was. They might speak about their anger at themselves, other family members or medical and nursing staff. They often give accounts of the important hospital appointments, the tests, the results, and treatment. They have sometimes become an expert on the medical condition of their loved one, some having a full understanding of all the processes and procedures. They will often speak about the reactions of the deceased, the frustration and loss of dignity that was experienced. In the instance of a sudden death, the story will be about what was happening up to the point of death. Most clients will want to talk about the final hours of their loved one's life, and how they died.

As we listen to these stories we hear the details that are important to the client, and we can often pick up some of the issues they are struggling with as they repeat certain phrases or go over again the particular aspects that have troubled them. Often these issues will be prefaced with words like, 'I don't know why they…' Or, 'I can't understand what happened.' Or, 'I can't get my head around it.' The story telling plays an important part in formulating an understanding of the events so that what has happened can ultimately be accepted. The first story might be about the illness but there are others that might be told, and they can come in any order. Stories will tumble out and somehow, as a collaborative piece of work, you and they need to put these stories into a 'whole' so that some semblance of structure can emerge. People will tell their stories in varying lengths and detail. Some will need many sessions before they are able to talk about the death.

Ron was in distress. His wife had died several months before he came to see me. He was an articulate and intelligent man who was now finding he was breaking down and wondering if he was going mad. He felt it was worse for him now than when his wife had first died and the initial months after her death, when he had things to do and sort out. The telling of his initial story started from his wife's last hospitalization and continued until a few weeks before her death. Ron couldn't, however, relate the last week of his wife's life; it was too painful for him to even contemplate. This was what he was struggling with the most, and he wanted to deal with it. He felt he couldn't go back to face it on his own because it was too overwhelming. But to talk about it would also mean he'd have to accept his wife's death. So I suggested he tell me the story of his wife's condition from the beginning, from the time of her diagnosis. She had been ill for many years, and Ron could remember in graphic detail all they had gone through so this story took us a few sessions to complete. Finally, when the story of her condition was told, only then was Ron able to tell the final story of how his wife died, and come to fully accept that she had gone.

How many stories might there be?

Figure 1.1 describes some of the stories that might be told. If we were to put them into chapter headings, some of the stories might appear under such titles as: 'When we first met'; 'Milestones along the way'; 'Happy times'; 'The gathering clouds'; 'Wider family influences'.

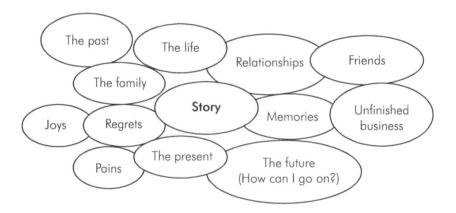

Figure 1.1 Stories to be told

One of the conclusions that can be drawn is that the potential for story telling is endless. The initial story might only be quickly told at the start of your sessions, or it may not. They will tell it in their own time, and they may return to it quite frequently. Many may feel they can not keep telling their story to their family, some of whom were part of the story and may not have been helpful. Clients sometimes feel they need to tell the stories to someone else outside the family, someone who has no history with them and no vested interests or hidden agendas.

Telling the story can come at any time in your meeting with a bereaved person. As you can see there can be many stories to be told and they do not all happen at once or in any particular order.

As we go through the different elements, there will often be an aspect of story telling. When you explore the relationship, for example, there will be stories told of what the deceased used to do or say, the funny things that happened, or illustrations of their particular ways. You may even hear about the dark side of the person that has died, if the bereaved person can allow themselves the opportunity to talk about this. After all, none of us is wholly good or wholly bad. When you are looking at celebrating the life of the deceased, there will be more story telling, and when they think through the legacies left behind there will be stories they want to share that illustrate what has been passed on and down to others in the family.

The way someone tells their story is important and can be helpful to the support worker in trying to understand what is going on for their client. What I mean is this: the way someone sifts the details of their story, the way they leave out or put in certain details can reveal much, if the listener is able to point this out to the client. You may need to ask something like:

> 'I didn't understand about... I wonder why that's so important to you.' Or,

> 'You didn't mention what happened after that. Wasn't that so important to you?' Or,

> 'When you told me about...I'm not sure, but you seemed to be quite... (e.g. tense, upset, confused, bewildered, angry, agitated, sad, or distracted). I wonder if that's right.'

Always be a little tentative about these comments as you might be on the right track or there might be another explanation. It has been my experience that if something becomes apparent to me in the way someone is telling their story, it can be profitable to explore it. You might get back something like, 'I didn't talk about…because I don't get on with… (name) and it makes me angry just to think about what they did.' You might then say:

> 'Am I right in thinking that you don't want to talk about that now, then?'

They can choose to talk about it or not, as they desire, but you have given them the option. Surprisingly enough, it might just be the moment they do choose to talk about that relationship or that event.

Components of a story

Many years ago I used to teach English, and it seemed to me the mantra of all English teachers was: 'Your story must have a beginning, a middle and an end.' I spent a lot of time helping the pupils to structure their stories and to plan them out. Inevitably I would receive their ramblings that would sometimes have good potential, if put in order. Most of us, I guess, do not have the type of brain that thinks through a structure of a story before we embark on the telling. Usually we start off at a certain point and make many detours, with punctuations of other thoughts, and explanations of other things and events that have happened, in order to explain the first part.

We especially might expect this to be the case after a death has happened. It is important to help people marshal their thoughts so that they and you can beneficially reflect on what they have said and how they have put it together. I sometimes find myself very confused about a client's story, the details seem mixed, the chronology does not make sense, so then I know I need to stop them and get them to clarify certain things, and to fill in the missing gaps. I might say:

> 'I'm not clear about the time frame here. What happened first?'

I find that if I do not have a mental picture about the major events in the client's story and the story of their loved one's diagnosis, treatment, or in a case of sudden death the events leading up to the death, then I feel less effective in my interventions. For the work of interpreting the story I can not make the connections I know are significant, as I am still trying to grapple with the overall picture.

So, it might be necessary to identify the components in the story for yourself, and take the client back to the places you have missed or were confused about. For me, it is important that the picture is complete. Don't be afraid to interrupt at times if you need clarification, and tell them it's important for you to get the facts right. I do assure the client about this: telling their story is important for them but it's also important for my processing. You can help the client by making such observations as:

> 'I'm not sure I'm getting the right picture here. Could you just go back to…and tell me about…?' Or,

> 'I'm not sure when that happened, was it…' (e.g. before she was diagnosed or after)?

When you notice that there are certain things happening in a story, like the repetition of certain words or certain details that come up again and again, it is useful for these to be reflected back to the client. Here's an example:

> 'I've noticed you've repeated this part of the story a number of times. It seems important to you. I wonder if there's something more about this you want to look at.'

People tend to get emotional when telling the story and when they are talking about the deceased we should be prepared for anything. As previously mentioned, Walter (1996) considers that it is not about bereaved people expressing emotions, but about talking about the person and finding out about who they were, like viewing a multifaceted diamond. I too have come to value the need the clients have to talk about their loved ones and explore what their lives were about and who they were. However, when the client is remembering the life of the deceased and their own involvement, at poignant times especially, the remembering almost always evokes emotional responses. In the telling of the story there may be emotions raised in both the client and yourself as the support worker. This can be a difficult place for both of you. Emotions,

however, cannot be avoided or ignored so they need to be acknowledged. This can be done while allowing the client to continue the story
and exploring who the deceased was in the fullest sense. You might need
to say:

> 'Something has really touched you as you're telling me about this.'
> Or,

> 'What you're telling me is very sad, and you're moved to tears by it. I
> wonder what's going on for you now.'

Checking with the client what is going on for them is helpful, to let them
know it is acceptable to feel the emotions and that you are not afraid of
what might come out. Often the client is afraid of crying and not being
able to stop, or speak, or carry on.

An important point to remember, however, is that what you are
hearing is only their view of the story. What you hear is the client's own
individual interpretation of events and happenings. If you think there is
possibly another side to this situation, it might be helpful to ask them to
imagine that someone else is talking. For example:

> 'If your daughter (mother, sister, brother, partner) were telling me
> this part of the story, what do you think she might tell me?'

It is advisable not to do this early on in the relationship of trust that you
are creating between you and your client, as they may feel you do not
believe them or you are not on their side.

If you are working with a person whose relative died suddenly or
tragically, you will need to take them through the story in minute detail,
over and over again. This is part of working with trauma. In the event of
a suicide there may be a relentless picking over the details, trying to
make sense of the events and seeing things with hindsight. Do not rush
them through the telling of these details; they may need months and
months of talking about the same thing. It is their opportunity to try to
piece the picture together and to try to come to an explanation for
themselves, one that they will be able to live with eventually, perhaps.
There may be others bereaved by suicide who may not wish to talk at
first, or at all, about all the details surrounding the tragic death. Allow
them space and do not push into the story, even if it seems unclear to
you, without asking them first. You may want to say something like:

'This has been such a painful time for you and I sense there is more to say about the events leading up to his death, but I wonder if you feel unable to go into any more detail at the moment.' Or,

'I sense this is perhaps too hard for you to talk about at this time. You may or may not want to talk about those things with me yet.'

Building up a relationship of trust is important and perhaps this client will feel safer after knowing you are not going to take them where they do not want to go.

THE MIDDLE STORIES

If you refer back to Figure 1.1 you will see how many stories can form the middle part of the whole. You might find yourself listening to stories about the family dynamics from years ago or in the present and you might wonder what this has to do with the bereavement. There has been some discussion as to what bereavement counselling or support actually covers. The question that is most pertinent for us is whether or not bereavement support takes into account previous history and struggles (Marshall 2007). Sometimes it may be relevant to do so and at other times you might find you are actually dealing with deeper issues than you are qualified to handle – at which point, it would be important to refer back to a qualified counsellor for an assessment of the situation. Getting supervision for your work is vital for helping to bring some clarity into the picture. We will discuss this further when we think about the impact listening to bereaved people can have on you.

Clive was a man in his forties whose father had died and who was very angry at everybody around him, not a surprising emotion at all for people in bereavement. However, after four or five sessions, the support worker began to feel uneasy about how Clive was using the time. After the initial story of his father's death, the sessions began to deal almost entirely with the problems around his marriage and his relationships with his in-laws. We understand that bereavement and grieving can often negatively impact other relationships in the family, but the support worker came to realize that these situations had actually existed before the death of Clive's father. The problem was more deeply rooted and would perhaps need the work of a qualified counsellor in general practice or a marriage guidance counsellor.

On the other hand, one might need to remember that the stories around family dynamics may well have a bearing on the bereaved person's adjustment to their changed life circumstances, and may need to be explored for those reasons. Do not automatically assume it is not in our sphere to explore these relationships because it is not immediately apparent how they relate to the bereavement or the grieving process. So be prepared to ask some questions, like:

> 'You've been talking a great deal about the relationships you have with your family rather than how it is for you in your bereavement. How do you think these relationships might be affecting how you're handling your grief?' Or,

> 'In the last few visits, I've noticed you've spent a lot of time talking about your mother-in-law and not about your father. I wonder if you're aware of that and could it be that we need to get back to talking about your loss?'

THE FINAL CHAPTER (CLOSING PARAGRAPHS) OF THE STORY

It might be useful here to pause and think specifically about a client you have seen. Cast your mind back to the time when they were telling you about the last days or hours of the life of their loved one. What were some of the important memories of this final chapter?

Mike's mother had died a few months before he came for support as he was experiencing loss of purpose. His life was a mess, he declared, and he hadn't got enough energy for any of it. Life hadn't gone his way since his mother had died, he felt, and there were lots of difficulties around work and family, so it took a number of sessions to get to the point of understanding what had happened at the death of his mother. He kept deflecting the support worker away from the death story, and they were dealing with the 'here and now' of his life for quite some time. The support worker got caught up in the process of trying to sort out how Mike might cope with everything and find some purpose again in his life.

When doing a review with Mike the support worker told him she still felt unsure about how Mike's mother had actually died and the details surrounding her death. Mike began to focus and started to tell that particular story. With encouragement, he spoke about the night before his mother died when the visiting nurse had suggested he might want to talk to his mother, to tell her things he might want to say while there was still time. Mike was surprised, but he spent some hours reminiscing with his mother even though she appeared to be unconscious. 'I didn't realize she was dying. I just thought she was sleeping a lot.'

It seemed that Mike had not really understood that his mother was dying and it came as a shock, a total surprise to him, despite the things that had been said and the signs that were being displayed. Over the past few months he had been living with the shock and disbelief of how his mother could have died. He said, 'I must have been denying it, or I hadn't heard it, but I missed the signs big time, didn't I?'

It was in starting to recall the small details of the final chapter or hours of his mother's life that Mike began to see things more clearly. That session with him began to open up the grief he had been struggling to express for the past few months. It was a starting point, not a finishing point, but one that came about because the support worker had taken him back to this event as she did not have the picture clear in her mind, and together they explored the final hours, not glossing over them but reliving them.

The unexpectedness of a death, shock and disbelief or even denial can play a big part in some people's stories and in the final events of the patient's life. 'He was such a fit man (woman) – why did it happen?' The unanswerable questions of 'why' can hang around the grieving process for many people. They can't understand how it could happen; it just doesn't make sense. When people die suddenly or even after a short time from the diagnosis, there is often a need to come to terms with the factual medical reasons. It seems the medical aspects around a death for some are a big feature in the last weeks or days of life. The way some people die can be very traumatic or complicated and not everyone, even in a hospice ward, will experience the quiet slipping away we would all hope for. There can be complications at the end of someone's life that mean the memory of the last days is almost unbearable for the grieving family.

Other things happen to patients in terms of their personalities, through medication or because of the disease itself, which mean the family might struggle with trying to have the ending they would want to have. Anne and her son Jim experienced some such difficulties at the end of Brian's life. He had been taken into the hospital but had started already to be different; his medical condition meant he was undergoing some personality changes. He was especially difficult with his son, Jim, abusing him verbally and trying to fight him physically. They couldn't understand this because he had never been like that in his life towards them. The memories his wife Anne was left with brought her no comfort; rather, she was experiencing nightmares about the scenes she had witnessed. Through the process of talking about it Anne was able to find a way of coming to an understanding that she felt made sense of it for her.

Sadly, medical mistakes can happen and the final chapter then takes on another meaning for the bereaved family. Elizabeth had spent the time before Steve died planning how she was going to battle with the medical authorities over the negligence that had led to her son's death. She had a good case and fought it for over two years. She was on an angry campaign; it became her mission to get justice for Steve. After it was over, however, she fell apart. From being a strong and capable woman fighting the cause for Steve, Elizabeth became weak and immobile, unable to do the simplest of tasks. She was finding it a struggle to adjust to a different life and hard to start to grieve for Steve and deal with the regret for the time she'd missed out on while he was dying. After a couple of years, Elizabeth needed to start all over again talking through her story and working on her own ways of responding.

Some deaths are plagued by family feuds at the end of a patient's life. This can leave some family members angry at what was said and done in the presence of the dying patient or just outside the ward door, when it should have been different. Others in the family may feel guilty and not be able to express it, or might not be able to apologize or ever feel they can make it up to the others for what happened, knowing that the loved one died hearing the row and the chaos. These are difficult situations and, sadly, the ones who need the support may not be the ones who ask for it. In the case of those who do, it is wise to help them see and own their part in the story and perhaps try to rewrite the ending. Sometimes they need help writing real letters of apology or of sadness to help heal the rifts. On the other hand, there can be times when families have been re-united around the bed and there has been reconciliation between some family members, so that the patient has been allowed to die in the knowledge that something good has taken place.

In your role as a support worker, what is your listening function while the story is being told? If you are a companion with someone on their grief journey, there are things you can do that will be useful and of benefit to them.

WHAT DO YOU DO WITH THE STORY?

> Key Listening Activity: Hear it and assist them
> to construct a bigger picture.

As we listen to the client's stories we want to enable them to tell their stories well; to assist them in constructing a bigger picture; to guide them in analyzing and interpreting their stories; and to support them as they rethink their past, and adjust to their present and future stories. The most important thing we can do when we visit those who are grieving is to listen. The listening skills of a support worker are, then, of paramount importance. Family and friends will offer advice, they will talk over each other, they will interrupt, and they will start to tell how it is for them. The bereaved person who has asked for support needs time devoted to them, their issues, their struggles and concerns, their own pain and sorrow.

In any preparation for bereavement support work, we concentrate a great deal on listening skills. We talk about 'bereavement support' rather than 'counselling' which makes people feel comfortable. We offer an opportunity to talk about their grief with a trained listener who understands some of the issues around bereavement. So the emphasis in our initial preparation for this work is on listening skills and how bereaved people might be experiencing their loss. There are many books devoted to the teaching and advancement of listening and counselling skills. I will therefore only discuss here the basic listening skills I think are necessary for bereavement support and vital at this particular point of listening to the story or stories the client wants to tell.

You can not empower people to construct a meaningful picture from the things they tell you if you can not recall what they have said, so remembering the details of someone's story becomes important in order to get a bigger picture of what has gone, or is going on for them. It is also important for you to make some connections with what they have said before. Of course, writing down some of these details after you have seen them will help you in the recall. You can assist this process by reflecting back what they have told you, which usually helps to fix it in your own memory. Reflecting back can help you recall the client's details, but it also helps them know you are listening. We can reflect back the **facts** of a situation and we can reflect back the **feelings** that seem to be expressed in their words.

Let's look at some examples that might come up in a bereavement conversation.

> *Carol*: We'd only had four years together before the illness struck and he was into the treatment before we knew what hit us. Everything happened so fast. We didn't seem to know what was going on really, or at least I didn't, looking back at it. Maybe Phil did because he used to say we needed to plan ahead and make sure everything was in order. I didn't want to know. I'd say to him, 'We're going to fight this together.' (Pause) I think I stopped him talking about it really.

> *Support worker*: You'd had four years together but this seemed to happen so quickly you didn't have time to take it all on board. **(Fact)** And it sounds as if you might be feeling some regret about not letting Phil talk about it. **(Feeling)**

> *Carol*: Yeah, I think I am really… It was a lot for us to deal with and we didn't expect it. So I didn't want to admit it was happening…that I might lose him.

> *Support worker*: At the time it seems you might have been struggling to come to terms with the fact that he might be dying. **(Feeling)**

It takes practice at reflecting, as some ways of reflecting are better than others – you don't want to become mechanical and parrot-like which sounds irritating and insincere. In the above conversation, the support worker is empathizing with the client and showing that she has understood the situation. The conversation opens up several avenues to follow, but only at the client's pace. You notice that the support worker picked up that Carol seemed to be sounding regretful. It was a tentative reflection of the feeling that might be there. You will notice too that she used 'regret' rather than 'guilt'. Guilt may have been too strong for Carol to admit to as this is perhaps a new thought for her, so regret 'feels' more acceptable. Carol agreed but went quickly on to talk about how much it was for them to deal with. The support worker went with where Carol was going. The support worker has used the words 'he might be dying' which perhaps Carol could not bring herself to use. There is a reality about death and dying which Carol admitted she had struggled with, so to use the words here helps her to face the reality.

The support worker will be able to return to the issues of the time factor. It is possible that Carol feels robbed of the time she and Phil should have had together, and maybe she will be able to admit to a deeper feeling of anger as she explores what's going on for her. Maybe the support worker will be able to talk later with Carol about the shattered dreams, the plans they had made together for their future that would not now come to be. The support worker may also be able to go back to the regret that Carol started to feel and explore it in more depth, because regret may start to feel like guilt, that she had robbed him and them of an opportunity for some special kind of intimacy at that time.

Let's revisit Mike (see page 47) when he began to talk about his mother's death and see how reflection helped Mike tell the story. The questions he had could have been a bit daunting but, with some appropriate reflection, more of the details of the story were able to come through for Mike and he was able to make some sense of what he was saying and what had happened.

> *Mike:* (Incredulously) I must have been denying it, or I hadn't heard it, but I missed the signs big time, didn't I?

> *Support worker:* You seem shocked that you could've missed the signs of her dying and that you might have been in denial. **(Feeling)**

> *Mike:* I couldn't have been taking it in, could I? ... I mustn't have wanted to hear or know. Was it just a hunch the nurse had about her? I just thought she was sleeping a lot, even though they told me she'd been taken off all her medication. (Pause) I should have known, shouldn't I?

> *Support worker:* You seem to be struggling with two things, the fact that the nurse seemed to know your mother was dying but you didn't; and the fact that you didn't realize taking her off her medication would mean she would die. **(Fact)**

Mike: No I didn't, you're right. Though at one level I suppose I did know. I obviously didn't want to know she was dying, so I must have brushed it aside. But I'm so glad the nurse told me to talk to her. I was able to say all the sorts of things I ever wanted to say. I told her how much I loved her and what a good mum she'd been, and how I respected her and appreciated all the advice and guidance she'd given me.

Support worker: So you're really grateful that you had time to say your final farewell and last words to her before she died. **(Feeling)**

Mike: Oh yes, I guess that was what they were, weren't they? I didn't realize at the time that was what they were, but I'm really glad I had that time with her before my sister and the others came.

Good reflection should enable the client to tell their story rather than take them off track. Summarizing skills, on the other hand, are a way of empowering your client to hear what they are saying for themselves and to choose what is important to explore. Summarizing is not making a list of all that has been said and relating it back mechanically, but rather getting the gist of what has been said and helping the client to focus. In her book on using counselling skills in palliative care, Jean Bayliss (2004) suggests that there are three main ways of summarizing which she defines as 1) contrast; 2) choice point; and 3) figure and ground.

In the extract below she uses an example of talking to a patient (p.81):

Contrast
After sensitive summarising of the material, the client is offered the possibility of working on contrast...

...(the summary), it seems as if on the one hand you'd like to be more welcoming to your visitors, but on the other there are times when you wish they'd stay away. Let's look at each in turn.

Choice point
After the summary, the speaker is reassured that everything they shared seems important, but which point would it help to focus on first. This helps the person to prioritise.

Figure and ground
If you look at the landscape or at a painting, usually something (the figure) will stand out from the (back) ground. Tentative reflection of

what seems to you to be the 'figure' can help focus. Being tentative is critical because the client must feel able to reject the suggestion.

> John, of all the problems you've shared with me, ——————
> seemed to stand out. If I'm right, shall we explore that first, and come back to the others?

I shall now apply these three options to a conversation with someone who has already spoken about how her husband was a hoarder of things, a model maker and a perfectionist. A summary of what she was talking about might sound something like this:

> *Support worker:* You've mentioned some of your husband's interests and his hobbies like model making. You seem to have admired his persistence in finishing jobs, though that could also be a little frustrating for you at times. And you've said you're finding it a bit tough going through his things including all the models.

It would be hard to know what the client might find useful to focus on, and you do not want to discount any of it. Using the three ways given above we can apply them to the summary we have given this client, so she can sort out what she wants to talk about.

Contrast:
Support worker: You've mentioned some of your husband's interests and his hobbies like model making. On the one hand, you seem to have admired his persistence in finishing jobs, though that could also be a little frustrating for you at times. And on the other, you've said you're finding it a bit tough going through his things including all the models.

Shall we look at them in turn?

Choice point:
Support worker: You've mentioned some of your husband's interests and his hobbies like model making, and you've thought about how you admired his persistence in finishing jobs, though that could also be a little frustrating for you at times. And you've said you're finding it a bit tough going through his things. All these things seem to be important. I wonder which one you'd like to talk about first.

Figure and ground:
Support worker: (After the summary) Of those things you've mentioned, sorting out your husband's things seemed to be the most

important thing you're facing right now. If I'm right, perhaps we
could explore that and then we can come back to the others?

As you identify for your client the areas they are bringing up, they will
begin to hear what they are actually saying and perhaps be empowered
to think through aspects of their stories for themselves. In empowering
them in this way, it is hoped they will be encouraged to construct a
bigger picture of their loved one and begin to see the wider view of their
loved one's life. But you will also want to guide them in analyzing and
interpreting their stories so that they might begin to rethink how they
have lived out their stories so far and how they might choose to go from
here. Analyzing can be difficult even for full-time students, so how do
you assist your clients to think carefully? One way is to ask open-ended
explorative questions, questions that help them focus on the story but
also the different characters in the story and the parts they played in the
life of the deceased and in their lives. One of the ways we support our
clients is in helping them think through how they might want to adjust
to their present and future stories as well as to rethink their past. Encourage imagination and analysis.

WHAT QUESTIONS CAN YOU ASK?

Reflect here on what questions you think you can ask that will focus on
the story the client is telling.

In asking questions, never appear too invasive or intrusive; people
need their space to think and reflect. At the same time, I have found
generally that most people love to talk about the one that they are
grieving for. In asking open questions we can help people focus. There is
often a state of confusion brought about by the grieving, but helping
your client to focus can bring them out of the 'fog' they sometimes feel
they are in. The type of questions you ask need to be open ended so that
the client can feel their own way in responding, either by jumping
straight in to tell wonderful stories, or to falter their way through some
painful memories. Below are some ideas we have come up with for
assisting people to tell their stories. These questions are not exhaustive;
there are many more. I would not suggest you use them as a
questionnaire to be worked through, but use them as a guide at first, and
I encourage you to think of your own questions as you listen to the

client. Remember to be a curious detective and find out as much as you possibly can and as much as they are willing to tell you.

- The story around the illness:

  > Tell me about what happened when he was diagnosed.
  > How did you manage during the months of the illness?
  > What were some of the biggest struggles for you at the time?
  > How did he seem to cope with his illness?
  > What kind of family support did you both have?
  > What kind of struggles did you have in the family around that time?

- The story of their life together:

  > Tell me about... (name). Tell me her story.
  > What was he like? (What sort of person was she/he?)

  (For a partner or spouse):

  > How did you meet?
  > What attracted you to him?
  > What kind of strengths did you find in him?
  > What will be some of your most important memories about him?

- The story others might have about the deceased:

  > What kind of friends did she have?
  > What sort of things have her colleagues at work told you about her?
  > What was his work life like?
  > How would he spend his spare time?
  > What did he like doing, as hobbies or interests?

WHAT TECHNIQUES CAN YOU USE?

We refer to these techniques as the 'tools' in our 'tool box'. Before we start, let me give a word of caution. It is important that you practise these techniques before you try them with a client and then you will know the pitfalls, or some of the things that might occur for the client. Also, do not think you have to use any of them. If a client is a natural talker, then you might not want to interrupt that flow, or distract them. So you would only use a 'tool' for a particular purpose. When clients seem to get stuck for something to say, or are not sure where to go in the conversation, are unfocused, or find it hard to start talking we might be able to use a tool to help them.

Photographs: Looking at photographs helps you to get to know the family; putting faces to names is often helpful in aiding your memory. It is also helpful for the client as a prompt to the story around that particular photograph and where the deceased was in their life journey. It also enables you to ask some questions to fill in the gaps in the story or build it up into a fuller picture.

This was once a real help to me when I was working with a particular client who just did not want to talk. He put up with me being there because he knew his family wanted me to see him. It was hard going and I began to falter; after all, there are only so many questions you can ask before you sound like a variation on the Spanish Inquisition. But thankfully there were some photographs of his wife around, and as they were there and he had not put them away, I felt I could ask about them. (Some people are not able to look at photographs for quite a time after the death, so it is respectful to ask about this before you start delving into the family albums.) I was relieved that he did open up and talk about the photographs and opened a window into their life together and their relationship.

It is a lot easier to encourage the use of photographs when you are in somebody's home because they are often around the walls or on tables and mantelpieces, or perhaps even in photograph albums, or drawers. But even if you are seeing them in another setting, it is still possible to ask them to bring in photographs for you to see. I have seen wedding albums, family albums and cardboard boxes brought in so that people can share their stories.

Some ways to talk about photographs might be:

> I see you have some photos up, are any of these of... (name)?

> I wonder if you would like to talk about it (the photograph) with me.

What was going on in the photograph? Where were you?

How did it happen to be taken? Who took the photograph?

Who are the other people in the photograph?

Was this before the diagnosis, or was it afterwards?

Three memory stones: I once went to a workshop where we were provided with a small drawstring bag in which there were three little stones. One was a smooth stone of a light colour; one a rough jagged one of a dark colour; and the third was a bright shiny and almost sparkly one. These little stones are to be held and felt. The smooth one represents some of the better times in the deceased person's life; the jagged one represents the darker more difficult times; the little gem is the one that represents the most precious moments that have been shared. When I did this exercise, I chose to talk about my father who died when I was nine years old, and I was surprised that all these years later I could recall so clearly some of the hard times, the good times and the precious moments, and was amazed at how they had the power to move me still.

You could make up your own little drawstring bag and find three stones to put in there, and it easily slips into a handbag, a briefcase or a jacket pocket, to be brought out at appropriate times.

Memory jars, memory books (life-story books), and memory boxes: Perhaps some of you will be familiar with these concepts in connection with children's work, but perhaps have not thought of suggesting them to adults.

Memory jars: With memory jars, you need: some salt; some coloured chalks; some scrap paper on which to rub the chalk into the salt; a little jar – the size of a kitchen spice jar is usually big enough for most people; and a piece of paper onto which to record the memories. You ask the client to choose probably about five or six memories of their loved one they want to put into the jar. The idea is to produce a jar that has strips of coloured salt, which looks like a jar you might have bought on holiday with wavy strips of coloured sand. You measure out some salt onto your scrap paper – a colleague of mine fills the jar first and then gets the client to pour out the salt into piles so that you get more or less the right amount of salt back in the jar. You ask the client to choose a colour for each memory and they rub the chalk into the salt until it is the right depth of colour needed for that memory. During this time they tell you about the memory and then pour the salt into the jar, moving it at angles if you want the wavy look. They record on the paper what memory each colour represents, so that in years to come they will remember it.

Just a useful tip – you need to make sure at the end that the jar is completely full to the brim and well packed down as you do not want each strip to merge into one another and end up with a sludge colour! Suggest your client keeps it upright at all times, too, for the same reason.

Memory books (or life-story books): At funerals these days it has become quite fashionable to have certain photographs either in a montage (collage type) display or in a book. The time is often limited, however, to produce one in time for the funeral, especially if family are scattered or photographs not readily available. So, if they have already done one, you can ask them if they would like to show it to you, and this can provide often a couple of sessions' worth of story telling. If they have not done one, then you can encourage them to think of doing one. I have found it is most helpful to talk to widows or widowers about this, using their children or young grandchildren as an incentive to motivate them. When children grow they forget and need prompting, so to have a book that can be brought out at special times, like a birthday or the anniversary of the death, is a way of remembering the deceased parent or grandparent. It can also be helpful for the adult children to do it for their own children and to involve their surviving parent in the project. This might be just what the surviving parent needs in order to think through the life of their spouse or partner and dig out old photographs and letters for their children and grandchildren's project. Big albums need to be found and plain ones can be decorated with children's creative work.

I remember working with Sam, whose wife had died several years before, and after quite a number of sessions, we got round to the subject of preserving the memories of his wife for her small grandchildren. He started by emptying the boxes of photographs they had collected and with the help of his daughters he selected the ones he wanted and tried putting them into chronological order. While all this was going on (it took a few months for it to be completed) the conversations he was having with his daughters were really significant for them all as they recalled the stories around the photographs. So, although I never did see the book, the work had been done at home and the stories were being shared, in the right place.

Memory boxes again might have been associated in your mind with children, but can be very special things for adults to prepare and keep. There may be letters and cards kept, there may be poems or other things written, or pieces of art work that can be gathered together and not lost and not distributed all round the house. Of course some people do want to leave these things around the house as it makes the presence of the loved one real in every room. But for those who can, this is quite a good way of bringing together those special treasures that can bring tears but also a warmth to the heart.

If people are able, they can bring these boxes out to share. Each object will have its story and reveal things about the deceased that you can comment on as you are impacted by the story and the object.

Journaling and letter writing: In a bygone era, a lot of people kept diaries and journals of their family and life events. In this fast track age, few of us seem to have time to do it. It was a practice that helped people reflect on the day's happenings, and perhaps helped them work out what they might do next or how they might respond in a certain situation. They would in effect do their own therapy on the written page. It might sound like a lot of hard work to suggest that your client starts writing, but for some (not all, by any means) it may prove to be a really excellent way of processing the events and helping them put things in order. At least it gives them the opportunity to think carefully about what happened.

Sometimes people experience difficult dreams. One of our clients had struggled with disturbing dreams and nightmares about her husband, and when her support worker talked about the content of these dreams in supervision it seemed the client might be revisiting the details of the final days and hours they had together through the dreams. My suggestion was that perhaps the client might be so afraid of losing the memory of her husband and those precious times that her mind was keeping them alive during her sleep. The support worker asked her client to try writing down the story of the last day and particularly the final hours and words. As she began to do this, a little at a time because it was so painful for her, she began to have better nights of sleep. When she got to the end of that story, she reported to her support worker that she was calmer, more rested, having better nights sleep, and felt able to put the book away in a special place. With the advent of personal computers, people can type out their stories, making it easier to do corrections when they find they have put things in the wrong order.

There are times when people are distressed at not having had an opportunity to say their proper goodbyes or to tell the person they loved them. This can happen due to the suddenness of a death when people have had no warning such as in a heart attack or an accident. Sadly, it can also happen in the case of palliative care patients because the dying person has kept the family from knowing how seriously ill they were, or the family and the patient were all in denial about the final outcome and did not address the concept of death. Letters to the loved one can be an outpouring of the heart and quite cathartic.

Letters might also be written that are not to a deceased one. These letters may still be of an emotional nature because they are dealing with a complaint, usually about the treatment of a loved one or the neglect of health professionals during the treatment procedures. These letters can be really hard to compose. There is a lot the bereavement support worker can do in acting as a sounding board for the client in the writing process. There may be many revisions to be done before the letter is sent, or it may be that the final decision is not to send the letter as they feel more reconciled with events and have worked through the anger.

Audio-visual: Those who are technically minded may be able to put together a visual recording of some of the events they had previously recorded of the deceased at family weddings, parties or holidays and these can be shown to the support worker and the family so that part of the life of the deceased is kept alive. Some people may find it hard to listen to the voice of the deceased and equally it may be difficult for them to watch videos, but for some people it is a wonderful project that is as effective as journaling.

Biographical story or life lines: When you encourage working on the biography your client can choose to do it either with the biographical details written out, or it can be done as a life line. I recall the first time I did this for my own life; I had drawn my life line as a map of the countries where I had lived. This gave me and the person I was talking to lots of material for reflecting on what had been happening for me in these places. So place and time can form quite an integral part of depicting the life of the deceased. People can be encouraged to use symbols that were meaningful to the deceased or put photographs onto it.

The life line can go literally straight across the page, using it 'landscape' rather than 'portrait' with high moments of the life above the line and low moments below the line. Or you can suggest they might want to represent it in any other way they choose. I have had clients use roads or rivers that wind around the page, or a series of steps or a stairway. A collage might also be made up that depicts the life of the loved one. Some of our clients are very creative naturally, and some can be encouraged to start using creative ways to help them remember and retell the stories. You can start this in the session with them or give them some ideas about it and see if they take it up. If you put it into the session, you will need to have large paper on hand and some coloured felt tip pens; the thicker ones are better for effect. People who have had a recent bereavement are less inclined to take this idea up, perhaps because it is too difficult to think it through, but it can be very helpful with people who are perhaps six months to a year further on from the death.

These techniques for your tool box are not exhaustive, but merely a few suggestions of how you might work with people more creatively; they need to be used wisely and judiciously. Not all people will want to get involved in some of the more creative things. You will know when they resist you, but don't be afraid to try. We never know when seeds have been sown and when they come to fruition.

I had suggested a life-story book could be done of Michelle's grandfather. She felt she needed to talk to her grandmother to get the details because she didn't know very much about her grandfather's life story. For two sessions Michelle came without the information and with what appeared to me to be excuses, so I explored with her what was going on and gave her a way of escape. 'Did it feel too much like homework?' No, she was sure she wanted to do it. One session a few months later she was full of talk about her grandfather's life. She had been to see her grandmother who had told her stories about her grandfather. Michelle felt her grandmother had really enjoyed talking about her husband and they had both shared a wonderful hour or two reminiscing.

It turned out that Michelle had worried that her grandmother would feel too sad to talk about her husband and that by introducing the subject Michelle would upset her. Instead she had found the opposite was true and there was now an opening for her to obtain photographs and stories and to invite her grandmother into the process with her. Whether or not the life-story book was completed in some ways is not the issue; the relationship between grandmother and granddaughter was deepened and the stories were shared about a colourful and fun loving man.

IMPACT ON YOU AS A LISTENER

At this point, you might want to take time to think through what struggles you may have experienced when listening to the stories your clients tell. Think specifically about a client you have seen. Cast your mind back to the time when they were telling you about the last days or hours of the life of their loved one. How did you feel when listening to the final chapter of this person's life? (How did it impact you?)

Listening to others' stories can be draining, especially when it comes to that 'final chapter' story. There will be times for us all when we get overwhelmed by one of the stories we hear. It is important to be aware of the way a story was told and the way it drew you in, or repulsed you, or distanced you from the client (and the dying patient).

I asked the bereavement team of support workers for some of their struggles; some of their responses were helpful for further exploration, so I will share them with you. Someone found they were indignant at the way the client was treated and felt a measure of the same anger at the medical staff as the client was feeling. A large number said they are often impacted by the sadness of the story and the tears shed by the client. Someone expressed puzzlement that certain things had been done which did not seem quite appropriate. (This led us into an interesting discussion of what might be appropriate for the client or not.) Someone expressed incredulity that his client was certain they had seen the spirit of the deceased leave the body. (This led us into a stimulating discussion about the paranormal and spiritual elements in our clients' lives.) Another said she felt distanced from the client, because she felt the client had over-dramatized the story and it felt unreal, more like a drama than a real event. Another had experienced disbelief and some measure of frustration at the denial shown by the client.

What we aim for is honesty in our exploration of the impact people have on us. Whatever the impact, it is good to take time to ask yourself how you have reacted or been impacted by this client or that one. We can often use how we are impacted by these stories to help us see something of how the client is coping or how they are relating to reality. It is also helpful to take it to supervision, especially if it has felt heavier than usual, or it has been an unusual response on your part which needs some discussion to help you.

In summary:

- As we listen to the client's stories we want to enable them to tell their stories well; to assist them in constructing a bigger picture; to guide them in analysing and interpreting their stories; and to support them as they rethink their past, and adjust to their present and future stories.

- Attempt to help the client construct a story that is bigger than the loss of their loved one. In this way they can review their part in their loved one's story and think about the continuing part they have in the future of their families and friends.

- The importance of the support worker being a listener and a companion, not an expert, is fundamental to our approach.

- One of the most important things we can do is listen well by reflecting the **facts** and **feelings** of their story. Help them think through the importance of what they are saying by summarizing well and enabling them to choose what is important to explore (remember: contrast, choice point, and figure and ground).

- Ask open-ended questions that encourage the deeper telling of the story.

- Use techniques or 'tools' only for specific purposes like focusing a client, or getting them started on a subject if they feel less able to talk about it.

CHAPTER 2

Element 2: There is a relationship

- ❀ There is a story
- ❀ **There is a relationship**
- ❀ There is a life to celebrate
- ❀ There is a legacy left behind
- ❀ There is a strategy for coping
- ❀ There is a journey undertaken

We have already addressed the fact that as human beings we love stories and especially stories about those we love. Our stories are crucially made up of characters, good, bad and indifferent. What makes a story compelling is the connection between each one of the characters and their relationships. An American psychologist, Larry Crabb (1987) wrote that as human beings we are fundamentally relational creatures: 'Like babies crying for the milk that sustains physical life, people desperately reach out for the kind of relationship that brings personal health' (pp.111–112).

If the relationships we seek play such a major part in our own personal health, then when a death of a particularly significant person occurs, it is no wonder we feel in ill health. It is also true to say that the nature of the relationship between the one who died and the one who is bereaved is a factor in the grieving process. Many relationships are imperfect. In fact, none are perfect: some are very good, some are fair, some are fiery and some are difficult. Whatever the nature of the relationship, the bereaved person may want to talk about the person who was significant to them, and they often need to be assisted in this. Sometimes they will want to make sense of the relationship. Sometimes they will just want to be helped to remember the good things about this person, so that the darkness does not close over the memories completely. Sometimes they will want to work through difficult aspects of that relationship. In exploring how they related to the deceased they may be helped to understand aspects about themselves, their own needs, their ways of relating, and perhaps the deeper meaning of that particular relationship to them.

Relationships are special to the two people involved, but other people were also involved in the life of the deceased person. In the previous chapter on story, it was deemed helpful for the client to find out from others about the deceased's life. This can be really helpful at the 'wake' after the funeral, where people who knew the deceased begin to share stories and their memories, which may not be known to the wife or children or parents of the deceased. However, sadly but naturally, those who were closest to the deceased may not be in a position to listen to those stories, or hear with any joy the memories that are being shared.

As the months go by in bereavement, silence can begin to close around the memories and stories. Members of the family or friends stop speaking about the deceased, as they think it will have an adverse effect. They see other members of the family crying and getting upset and so they do not want to talk about things that might be painful. Friends may feel that to talk about the deceased might stop people moving on; they may begin encouraging them to start making a new life. It sounds to the bereaved person as if the relationship has to be filed away somewhere, and forgotten. Misunderstandings of how people grieve can come into play. The concept that is being given credence here, without realizing it, is that the bonds with the loved one should be broken and detachment should take place. Where does this thinking originate and what is so wrong with it?

The concept of 'breaking bonds' with the deceased after a death was popularized through the work of Freud at the beginning of the 20th century. Stroebe *et al.* (1996) wrote, 'Freud saw the psychological function of grief as freeing the individual of his or her ties to the deceased' (p.33). Before Freud's work, people demonstrated their grief openly and lived with the pain of broken hearts. The problem I have with Freud's theory and the work of the past century on detachment is that it does not seem to match the reality of bereaved people's experiences. Stroebe *et al.* cite research involving a sample group of young widows and widowers providing evidence that in their experience the bonds are definitely not broken. Among other things, it was found that 'the deceased continued to have strong psychological influences over the way the widowed organized and planned their lives' (1996, p.39); and in fact many of the bereaved people would still 'consult' the deceased over major decisions.

So, using that research to inform our practice, we must be careful not to direct people towards 'letting go' or breaking the bonds with the loved one. We need an approach that encourages them to explore their relationship and to value it, and we need to respect what they want to do with the relationship. Allowing the client to direct you would be a good starting point. From the above research findings we can say that many people's relationships continue after death and it is important to honour that continuing bond without suggesting that the ties be cut.

Where do people who want to talk about their loved ones go when they can not talk to their closest friends and family? It can be a lonely and solitary place anyway after a death, but it can be made even more solitary by the inability to talk about and discuss the one who has died.

At this point, pause to reflect on what people who have been bereaved have wanted to tell you about their relationship with the deceased. (What aspects, what stories, what memories?)

Many people want to talk about their relationship during the illness and how it changed their relationship completely. Some struggle because of the indignity of the illness, and their lasting images of their loved ones, often so changed by the monster of the cancer or the disease. If they saw the deceased after a tragic accident, they are often left with that image. The outward appearance may have been so altered that the image remains a haunting spectre, to be exorcised before they can begin to recall again the face and image of the healthy person. You may hear, 'All I can see is the way he looked at the end (during the last phase of the illness, or after the accident). I don't seem to be able to see him as he was when he was well. I don't want to remember him like this, but I can't get past it.' Time talking over the details of the illness or the accident, and gentle invitations to talk about their relationship will be supportive.

The illness may have taken away the 'person' before the death occurred. In many instances the place of the relationship between man and wife was substituted for a patient/carer (or nurse) role. In the same way, the relationship of parent and child can be affected in a long-term illness with both adult and young children performing many roles of a nurse, a parent or a carer. The relationship was changed, the power balance became different. For the partner, the relationship of equality was lost and the one became dependent on the other; and for the child, the responsibility for the care of a parent will have reversed the natural order of their life.

It could be quite beneficial to help the bereaved person explore this change of relationship. Our natural instinct, however, might be to try to reassure the client, brushing away their fears or concerns by saying things like, 'I'm sure you did all you could.' Or, 'That's in the past now, you've got to look forward.' It is possible to be in too much of a hurry to get past this place of pain, and that may be because we do not want to lead the client into something that feels too dark and painful for them – and us. But the client may need to linger over the things they did for their loved one; the way they spoke or were spoken to; the way they felt frustrated or even got angry with their loved one when things went wrong. Tiredness, exhaustion, emotional pain, anxiety and fears all play their part in altering the way people relate to each other at these stressful times. The client may well want to rethink how they or their loved one responded. You might want to say something like:

> 'You seem to have been aware of a change in your relationship as the illness progressed. I wonder if you'd like to talk about that in more detail.'

This might open up the way forward for them to explore how it had changed. You might be able to follow on with something like:

> 'How did that affect your closeness?' Or,

> 'What got in the way of the special relationship you shared?'

Peter had gone through such struggles when Shirley seemed to have a change of personality and was no longer the woman he thought he knew. She occasionally called Peter by another name, and she began acting in a way that was unexpected. Shirley became quite distant with Peter and he was left wondering what had happened in their marriage. The last weeks and days were of little comfort to him and he had to handle the sense of betrayal, real or imagined, before he could get back to the good memories and hold on to the years of happiness they'd had. We compared Shirley's behaviour before and after the medication and treatment. I asked:

'How would you've expected her to respond given her usual behaviour towards you and the physical affection you often shared?'

This helped him to begin to think through some specific stories and occasions which we could then reflect on. It would not have been helpful to say to him: 'I'm sure there wasn't anything at all to worry about. It was probably the medication that changed her and the way she spoke to you. It can happen in these cases.' In fact, he might have found that patronizing and he might have clammed up. I am also not qualified to give an opinion that is a medical one and, although I have heard of such things happening before, it would not have been useful at that point to tell him this.

Sometimes people have felt the invasion or the intrusion of the teams of professionals who seem to have taken over the house. The different nursing teams might have come in to bath, change dressings and give advice; a specialist nurse offering support and acting as a go-between with the doctors and hospital; and many others who might have trooped through the door on a regular, if not daily basis. This may have taken its toll on the relationship and may need to be explored. Some have told us of the way they became jealous of the relationship their partners had with the nurses. They struggled over the way their partners seemed to be brighter with the nurses, but when they were on their own things were different. It seems in these situations that the nurses were sharing the details of the illness and the partner trusted them. This presents a real struggle for the client that is hard to articulate for fear of being judged. The kind of help the nurses could provide was necessary and so they had to overcome this emotion. Often if they tried to talk about it with their partners they would argue and experience uncomfortable silences.

The regret and sorrow clients feel afterwards about that time need to be explored. It would not be helpful to say, 'It was natural for you to feel jealous, I might also have done in your place.' Or, 'I'm sure he didn't really want to cut you out, he was putting on a good show for the nurse.' If we try to explain away the behaviours, the client's or the deceased's, the client will counter our explanations. They may also feel you do not understand what they are really struggling with. What they want to explore is the state of the relationship at that particular time: the loss of intimacy, the tensions created, the words thrown at each other, the feelings of betrayal and so on. It may well feel like hitting a brick wall to the client, as they try to get past these memories to go back to better memories and to the place where they can start to celebrate some of the wonderful things about their loved one. So instead of trying to make it feel less important, it is better to say to a client in this situation:

> 'It was really hard for you to share… (name), particularly with the nurses.'

Acknowledging their struggles will help them to go as far as they want to go with it. You might be able to say:

> 'You wanted the kind of relationship you'd always had with him but he didn't seem to have enough energy. He seemed to be shutting down on you.'

Saying these things can help them acknowledge the pain of the situation in a non-judgemental way. It could also help them begin to see the situation more realistically.

There are, of course, other areas of the relationship to explore with the client. Again, like the story, their relationship had a beginning. There was a time when two people came together and their lives were moulded differently. They related to and impacted on one another. When a partner dies, the bereaved person may struggle to make life work again without the other, so life has to be relearned. When a parent dies, the adult child recalls the type of relationship they had and the influences their parent had on them. Sometimes this is difficult and may need careful handling because the memories may be painful ones rather than happy ones. After the birth of a baby, the parents are affected and life changes forever. When that child dies, the parents have to redefine their roles and their relationship; the surviving parent or parents relive their past years with the child. If the child became an adult, they think perhaps about the life their adult child carved out for themselves and the changing nature of their relationship.

Whatever the relationship, the beginning of it can be explored, and the impact that the deceased person made on your client can be discovered. You can open up the discussion with simple questions or requests that invite the client to talk about the relationship.

With the loss of a partner or a spouse, you can say:

'Tell me about how you met and what attracted you to him.'

With the loss of a parent you can say:

'What was your mother like as a person?'

'What are some of your early memories of her?'

With the loss of a child you might want to start with:

'What sort of baby and toddler was he?'

'What sort of things did he do that made you laugh or smile?'

What you are enabling the partner, the child or parent to do is to share their loved one with you in a way that others in the family will not require or allow them to do. This is an opportunity for them to explore who the deceased was, and how they related to them. You might want, of course, to explore how the deceased related to others in the family and there may be some funny stories and there may be some difficult ones, but the client has the choice of editing what they want to say to you.

In sharing about the relationship, you will undoubtedly find yourself back in the story-telling element. There will be stories about shared occasions, holidays, Christmases, birthdays, and so on. In these stories the client will be telling you something about the nature and character of the deceased. Ask yourself:

'What do I learn about this person from this story that I might share with my client?'

Then tentatively offer your observations to the client. You may enhance the picture they have of their loved one and they may come to a deeper understanding of that person for themselves.

Because relationships have their own specific dynamics, and because the relationships between family members and the one who died are different, I will deal with some of these separately. In looking at the relationships, I will be exploring some of the difficulties I have come across that have affected the way people grieve.

DEATH OF PARTNER OR SPOUSE

As discussed previously, during the time of illness there may have been the loss of intimacy, physical and sexual as well as emotional. The physical nature of the illness may well have meant that it was no longer possible to enjoy the sexual side of the relationship, nor even the small caresses of lovers because of the body's low pain threshold. And even if the sexual act were possible, sometimes the healthy partner might have been afraid of inflicting pain, or making demands, or felt guilty about even thinking along those lines when the partner was ill. Intimacy is expressed in different ways and it might be that they experienced a deeper level of emotional intimacy during the illness.

In the case of sudden death, or a suicide, the relationship was suddenly and brutally taken away. There was no time for adjustment to the idea of separateness and loss. The loved one was torn away from the client and the relationship abruptly ended. There was no chance for last words, for petty arguments to be resolved, or for declarations of love and affection. Listening to clients in these circumstances might mean helping them talk through their own issues of what the relationship was in their minds and perhaps what it might have been to the one who died. After a suicide, they might experience anger at the betrayal of their love and deep hurt that their relationship was not enough to live for. After death there is the empty bed, the aloneness and the aching void to be endured. We will discuss this further on in Chapter 7 when we look at difficult subjects to talk about.

In some cases there is a loss of truth and honesty between partners or spouses because of denial on one or other's part as to the extent of the illness or the seriousness of it. This could have deeply impacted their relationship. If both people were in denial, then perhaps they colluded to keep up the pretence. But often we will hear that there was an element of play acting, or putting a brave face on, when actually they knew what the reality of the situation was, but neither could face talking to the other about it. This can come from a real desire to protect the other partner from any more pain than is necessary. A deep feeling of aloneness might have been experienced which lingers on after death in the deep regret of not having been able to face the truth together. The surviving partner can experience distress at the lost opportunities in the face of death. They start to agonize over what they could have done, said and shared together. If the healthy partner was the one denying the reality of the imminent death, often they will struggle afterwards with not helping their partner to say the things they could have said.

Exploring the guilt and self blame that might arise can bring about some thought provoking and perhaps life changing approaches to illness and death in the future. They might on the other hand experience some anger at their partner for not telling them the truth so that they could have been more prepared. You might hear, 'Why didn't he tell me the truth? I could have handled it better then. I wouldn't have been so irritable with him if I'd realized what was going on for him.' Their anger can also be tinged with guilt about the last days and their relationship difficulties, such as bad temper and cross words.

As a support worker you will need to be careful not to say things like, 'I'm sure you didn't mean it. After all you didn't really know he was dying, did you? You can hardly blame yourself now for what you did then.' This may be what you are thinking but it is not helpful for the client, who needs to wrestle with the consequences of their actions and words, working out for themselves how to respond in the light of what they now know. Significant support happens when you reflect what the struggle is and then explore the relationship with the client. It might be better to say something like:

> 'You're struggling with the fact that you didn't realize he was dying. And if you'd known, you might have been able to say and do some different things.'

You might be able to follow this, if it is taken up, by asking:

'What sort of things would you have wanted to say or do?'

It might take them a while to think through what they would have wanted to say, but it also might open up the chance to suggest that they write some of those things down after you have gone and give it some serious and significant thought. Acknowledging their struggle with not 'knowing' about the imminent death might also bring about a response that surprises you. They might actually tell you that they think they really did know, down in the depths of their being, and they didn't want to give voice to it with their partner. You can then go back to what they might have wanted to say or do. Sometimes the 'unsent letter' is a good way to help people deal with their regrets at not saying the things they have still retained in their hearts and minds.

The client's own emotional well-being feels crucially linked to the relationship that is being mourned. The loss is centred on missing the relationship that was unique to them. A problem for some bereaved spouses or partners is that they are not able to admit that someone else in the family can be hurting as badly as they are. Marjorie was a case in point. She had two adult sons who were both married with their own children. 'They can't be hurting as much as I am,' she would say. 'They've still got their wives and children. I've lost my husband. How can they be as miserable and hurting as I am?' Marjorie's world had revolved around her husband; her sons had left home years before and had made their own lives. Whatever had happened in the past, she felt disconnected from them at this time and could not identify with them in their loss of a father. Only the loss of her relationship with her husband mattered to her.

With a client like this it would be natural to struggle with her response, thinking she is being self-centred, and feeling perhaps vaguely critical of her. You might feel like saying, 'Yes, but they have still lost their father and they have their own grief to go through.' You might want her to face up to her 'wrong' way of thinking. But she will not react well to such a challenge. So it might better to say:

> 'You're really struggling with your own pain and finding it hard to think they can be hurting as much as you are, because you've lost your husband and they've still got their wives.'

It might take weeks and months until someone like Marjorie can think about their children's grief without comparing it to their own.

DEATH OF A PARENT AS AN ADULT

There is a specific group of adults who struggle after losing a parent. This could be for many reasons, too complex to explore here, but there could be a very close relationship that leaves the adult feeling the pain of loss and the real sense of being orphaned. Sometimes this makes people aware of what it means to face their own mortality. It could also be that now the adult child has to face growing up. Where parents have helped make decisions and have played a big part in supporting the child through adult life, the adult child has now to face life alone without the parental guidance.

Tina's relationship with her mother had been her life line in an unfulfilled relationship with her partner. Her mother kept her going when things were bleak at home and at work. Her mother was her confidante and her 'rock' and she had been bereft; there was no one to turn to anymore. However, she also was afraid of what it meant to be without her. She didn't feel prepared emotionally or mentally to be alone out there in the universe. (Her father had not been able to support Tina, being wrapped up in his own grief.) She had talked about some of the significant people in her life that had moved away or had retired from work.

> I made a simple observation, 'It seems to have been important for you to have an older person to look out for you. I wonder what that's about for you.'

She was able to start unpicking the relationship between herself and her mother and was gently helped to see that she could become the adult, and not remain the child who was continually looking for someone to rescue her. She was able to begin to come to terms with life without a mother or a substitute, sad as it is, and she made a start in realizing she would have to live with the sorrow of this without being stunted by it.

There are some relationships that have been difficult throughout life, and the adult child has wanted the relationship to be deeper and more loving, but the parent has not been able to give what the child wanted. Simon, who had been the youngest child, would never be able to get what he had longed for from his father, his approval and his unconditional love. His father had withheld these from Simon ever since he could remember. Simon never knew why and now he never would know, nor could he work to improve the relationship. His father had been critical and demanding of his son all his life and yet Simon had tried so hard to please him. His words still had the power to cut the adult Simon down to eight years old, despite the fact that he held a responsible position at work. Exploration of this and the freedom to express his anger and guilt were helpful. All this helped him to put the past relationship into a different place, seeing it as something beyond his understanding but also out of his control. He wasn't 'healed' from the pain, but neither was he carrying it around as something that could come up and hit him when he least expected it. He also started to review his relationship with his own children and found it helpful to be reminded of what could be detrimental for them.

Some adult children struggle after a parent has died because the relationship with their parent was too close. They are often the ones who say, 'We were like sisters. She was my real soul-mate.' These relationships sound wonderful, but in truth they may be too entangled. This might be for many reasons, some possibly linked to other unsatisfactory relationships (their marriages or partnerships), and so they have found themselves very close to each other and have not been able to detach. Or it might be that they had not detached when the child was growing up, and in teenage years had formed the bond that could not be broken and perhaps which neither wanted to break.

It is really difficult to suggest to these people that they were perhaps too close to their parent, as that would sound like sacrilege to them. So you can only explore the relationship and perhaps ask:

> 'How did the relationship with your mother impact on other relationships in your family?'

This might bring up stories of sibling rivalry or jealousy, and it might also get you close to the subject of how their partners might feel about the relationship. With these clients, you are allowing them to explore the web of relationships that surrounded this one and the impact of this relationship on their life. We should remember, however, that they are struggling to come to terms with the loss of this relationship and you should try to avoid any hint of criticism about it.

In those relationships where there has been a period of caring for the parent during a time of illness, there can be real issues for the surviving adult child about the reversal of roles that took place, where they assumed the parental role, particularly perhaps for those whose parents suffered from dementia in old age. The caring role and the parenting role is one that helps to fulfil significant needs in us in the face of felt helplessness against the illness. When this role is over there is a huge void, a lack of purposefulness which needs to be addressed.

You could ask:

> 'You had a very important role as carer for your mother. What might life look like now for you after the loss of your role as a carer?'

This may help the person think through how they are going to make the adjustment. It is a question that should be asked after you have established a working relationship and they trust where you are coming from. You are not trying to hurry on the process and get them to start doing things (as some of their family members might be doing). But you are asking it in a way that does not avoid the obvious fact that they had a role and it is no longer there any more.

Some people get on with life by adjusting to the new freedom, and some people find that the new found freedom is their enemy. Some people feel a sense of relief that the battle is over and the parent has been released from the fight, but then feel guilty for feeling relieved. Some people get focused on the way their parent died, and find it intolerable to think that the parent would have been in pain. For those who died in hospital after an operation or after an accident there can be real fear that this was the case. It can be just as difficult for those who had to endure watching and waiting for a parent to give in finally after a prolonged deterioration in a life limiting illness. For these clients, it may be of benefit to have an opportunity to speak to a doctor or nurse who was involved in the care of their parent. I have witnessed the immense reassurance for some people, and not only those whose parents have died. It has meant they have been able to grieve in a more constructive way after some of their questions have been settled.

For some adult children, the parent died too soon. The middle aged parent of an older teenager, for instance, leaves the barely adult person in some difficulties. It is hard enough to be 18, 19 or 20 without having to cope with the loss of a parent as well. These young adults are hard to reach, as they tend to want to struggle with life by themselves; after all, they're adult now, aren't they? They may withdraw from their family members and try it alone – in which case, they will not appear for support until something else goes wrong in their lives, and even then they may not necessarily associate the cause with the loss of their parent. If you are a counsellor in private practice or in a doctor's surgery you might be meeting these people in their late twenties or early thirties presenting with self-destructive behaviours. They may be self harming, or in serial abusive relationships, or be drug or alcohol dependent and they may have employment difficulties and/or a criminal record. They may have dropped out of university or work and do not appear to have much purpose in life. The immediate problem will not appear to be bereavement. But perhaps a little exploration will show that there might be unexpressed grief and anger around the death of a parent. They may also have 'lost' the other parent too, as the surviving parent struggled with their own grief, withdrawing into their own world or another relationship. The parent may have made the assumption that the young person did not want to talk or was coping; they may not have realized that the young adult was screaming inside and could not handle their grief appropriately. Sometimes the surviving parent remarries quite quickly, and the young adult is left out of the newly found happiness still grieving for the dead parent.

It is unfortunate that we can only support these young people when they are ready to ask for help. They will then probably want to talk about their parent and try to understand the relationship they had. Perhaps they will have 'sanctified' the deceased parent and not be able to see them in real life terms as a parent who was human with weaknesses and faults. Pointing this out at an opportune time might help the client see what they are doing:

> 'I hear so much that is wonderful about your mum, and she sounds as if she was a lovely person. But you know, I've never met the perfect person…you know, the one without any faults, and I'm wondering if Mum had any of those human flaws that we all suffer from.'

There may still be reticence to share at that level, but there may also be the beginning of building a realistic picture of the parent.

One of the difficulties for the young adult is that the relationship with the deceased parent did not have time to mature and was still in the formative and often tense stages. Perhaps the decisions the parent made were the wrong ones and the young adult is still angry. As we become adults we can see that things were less black and white than we might have thought in our idealistic years. There are, of course, some relationships that have been really difficult, and the young adult now has to come to terms with the abusive nature of the parent/child relationship that again did not have time to grow through the more turbulent years of their teenage life. Some teenagers or young people might be afraid they are going to turn into their abusive parent, or 'inherit' a drug or alcohol problem. Sensitive exploration about this difficult relationship will be vital.

DEATH OF AN ADULT CHILD

In the natural order of things, no parent expects to be standing at the graveside of their child or having to scatter their ashes. The natural order of life has been violated and turned upside down when a child dies before their parent. Betty's daughter, Beth, died in her late twenties. Beth had been ill for some time, but had managed to live reasonably independently for a few years. In the final stages of her illness she was in and out of hospital, and Betty was there for her daughter round the clock. But there wasn't enough time. Betty, who had spent years working hard as a nurse, had decided to take early retirement to be with her. Beth died a few weeks into Betty's retirement and Betty was devastated, her life shattered.

After the telling of the story of Beth's illness and her stays in hospital, we talked about Beth's life and their relationship. Through our conversations, Betty relived some of Beth's past years and the time she'd spent with her children and especially Beth, on their holidays. Betty's struggle was the regret and sorrow she now felt that she'd spent all those years working and not enough of the time with her children. In a situation like this it might be helpful to say something like:

> 'Your regret seems to be that you worked and didn't have more time with your children. You can see that now looking back, though at the time you had no idea of the way things would change.'

From what I had gathered in the way she spoke about Beth, Betty seemed particularly fond of Beth. So I made that observation:

> 'From what you're telling me, Beth seems to have been a sensitive person and quite special in your affections.'

Just this simple observation meant that Betty was able to talk more about how Beth had been more sensitive and caring towards her mother and had made time over the years to be with her, especially as Betty had been a lone parent from the time Beth had been a teenager. Betty's other daughter and son hadn't appeared to be so caring of her and when they'd left home they'd become more distant.

Parents need the time to think about the life their adult child carved out for themselves and to think through the changing face of their relationship. Betty went on to share how Beth's life had been a rollercoaster and particularly difficult, and she hadn't been able to share much of that part of her life because of certain choices Beth had made. Beth's life might not have been what Betty would have wanted for her daughter, but I was able to help her focus on who Beth was, the personality she was and the relationship they'd built up, especially during her illness. I did wonder out loud with Betty:

> 'I wonder if your relationship got closer over that period because Beth became more dependent on you – as if you'd got a second chance to take care of her.'

Sensitive communication needs careful editing of what you say and how you say it, but if you go with what they have given you, without making assumptions, you may be on target. However, there are some things you can leave hanging in the air. I did not say it to Betty, but I wondered if, in a terrible way for her, she felt the wrong child had died. Sometimes it is wise to keep your own counsel.

Sadly, it is of note that where they have experienced the death of a child, many partnerships and marriages do not survive because of the isolation that comes between the grieving parents.

DEATH OF A SIBLING

Betty's other children had not requested support, perhaps they were genuinely too busy to take on board the enormity of the loss of a sister, or perhaps their relationship had not been as close as it might have been, or perhaps they were well able to process the loss and still function in their own demanding lives. I can only hazard a guess. But there are times when it is really difficult for the brothers and sisters left behind after a sibling has died. They were perhaps sidelined while the child, adult or young, was ill, while mother and father were running backwards and forwards to the hospital, or nursing the child at home. The surviving siblings can feel they have been kept out of the picture by parents who have been too busy or unable to relay the details of what is happening to their other children. The surviving siblings may feel guilty at the anger they experience at their parents. Being the child left behind may be really stressful and deeply affecting. The grieving parents are struggling, yet there are remaining children who are living their lives and wanting to go on to achieve, to be successful and wanting recognition from their parents for their achievements. Sometimes the siblings feel the guilt of being left behind. They can feel that they can never do enough to make up for the child who has died.

Evan was in his twenties when his older brother died. It had been a shock for all the family; how could such a vibrant young man be struck down? It's not supposed to happen like that. While his brother was going through his treatments, Evan was trying to pass his accountancy exams. He experienced a mixture of emotions: his brother was dying but at the same time he was trying to make a success of his life. He felt guilty; it felt wrong for him to be focusing on himself, but he had to pass the exams as his job depended on it. He wanted to have a social life too, so he grappled with wanting to be with his brother and his parents but also wanting his own life. After his brother's death he took on the weight of his parents' grief; even though in his head he could rationalize that he wasn't to blame for his brother's death, and he wasn't to blame for his parents' sorrow, yet emotionally he carried that huge burden.

It would be useless trying to come at this from a rational point of view. Of course, Evan knew in his head he was not to blame, but the guilt of being the surviving child remained.

> 'How does your brother's death impact on your position now in the family?'

This was a question I asked early on in our sessions and was very surprised when I got the response, 'It's like the wrong child died.' Whether this was right or wrong, whether this was what his parents really felt, and I am sure they actually did not, this was Evan's perception, because of the way he felt they had kept much of what was going on with his brother from him. In my head, I was thinking that they probably hadn't wanted to apply any more pressure to him than he already had at that time, and I supposed they would have wanted to protect him. However, this was Evan's perception of the way it was. How do you respond sensitively so that he can explore the issues himself? I tried:

> 'That sounds really sad. I wonder where that thought is coming from.'

We went on to talk about his difficult relationship with his mother and the close relationship he thought she'd had with his brother, so he imagined she would have preferred to have his brother around. Our conversation helped him think it through a little. At a later stage I was able to ask about how it might have been for his parents if he'd been the one to die and his brother had been left. These situations are extremely difficult as you have to wait for some of the processing to take place in order for the thinking to change.

WHAT DO YOU DO WITH THE RELATIONSHIP?

> Key Listening Activity: Explore the relationship to bring out meaning.

Exploration means being a detective without being pushy or intrusive. The quality of your active listening becomes important here. As you have listened to their stories and have come to understand a little about some of the family dynamics, you can use what you have gained to explore the relationships that have existed around the deceased and the client. If you have been involved in the family before, as a nursing practitioner doing a follow-up bereavement visit with the family, do not assume you know what the relationship was about before you entered the story. It will still be helpful to the client for you to explore how they were before the illness took over their lives. 'I knew him in the time of the illness, of course, but tell me about him before then. What was he like?' This may be all you need to say to help the client start thinking about times before the illness, and perhaps a prompt to them that they can actually think back to those times. I understand that time for these visits might be limited, but it is my experience that you can do something at this point that will be beneficial and meaningful to the client. If you have time for regular sessions, you can build up a picture of the deceased and the relationship they had within the family by asking some simple questions and being curious.

As we explore the relationships we try to bring out the meaning of the life and of the relationship. Our exploration is not about curiosity for its own sake, but it is about helping the client build up a bigger picture of the life of their loved one and the way that life impacted them. You might explore the things they had learnt from each other and what the relationship had given to each one of them. You might explore where the relationship was strong and where it had failings. You might explore where they had struggled together and how they had sorted out their differences. The exploration is sensitive, but it can go into areas that family and friends might not touch.

WHAT QUESTIONS CAN YOU ASK?

As we talk with people in a sensitive way, we need to be sure that we are not being so inquisitorial that people feel as if they are being bombarded. On the other hand, we want to be interested and curious about the loved one. It could be quite important to the client that you remember certain things about the deceased, as it would mean that the person was memorable to someone else outside the family.

So, as an attitude, be curious about the deceased, their relationship, the relationships with others in the family, outside friends and work colleagues. Remember, good questions are open ended, rather than closed, so that you don't get just a yes or no response. An example of a closed question would be, 'Did he have a lot of friends?' It could get the response, 'Yes' or 'No', and may not get you much more. Instead, try this open question:

'What sort of friends did he have outside the family?'

This may get you a description of a lot of people of different kinds or a group of people of a certain kind. How fascinating it is to find out about the kind of people who were involved in the deceased's life and what made them get along together. So here are a few questions to help you get started on exploring their relationships.

- *For spouses and partners:*
  What were your early days of marriage like?
  How would you describe him as a person?
  What would you say you appreciated most about him?
  How did you handle those disagreements and conflicts that happen in any relationship?

- *For parents:*
  What kind of child was she?
  What sort of things did he enjoy at school?
  What were some of his strong points and some of the things he struggled with?
  How did he relate to you while he was growing up?
  What kind of woman did she become?
  What was your proudest moment as his parent?

- *For adult children at the death of a parent:*
  What kind of parent was he?
  What do you remember of your childhood with her as a parent?
  Who did the disciplining when you were at home?
  How did your relationship change as you left home and began independent living?
  What did you appreciate most about your mother?

- *These questions might be generally applicable:*
  What sort of things did he do that made you laugh or smile?
  What kind of holidays did you have together (or apart)?

What kind of things did you do together?
What interests did you have in common?
In what ways would you say you were different?
What have friends said about her?
What did she mean to her friends?
What stories have friends got to tell you about him?
How did your relationship change when the illness took over?

WHAT TECHNIQUES CAN YOU USE?

Here are a few tools for the tool kit, but remember that you will only use these tools if someone is unable to talk about things or if there are things that need to be sorted out, or someone needs focusing.

Family tree: In these days of blended families, some families will have very complicated connections. I remember working with a client whose father had died, and whose family was most complicated, as there had been two marriages and some other relationships that had produced children. My client was quite involved in the family so I started to do a family tree with him. This was initially so that I could have a better picture of them as a family, but it became really helpful to him. As we started to build up this family tree he was recalling the stories about the various members of the family, which enabled me to ask about how they related to his father. It brought up some realizations about his family and as I started to circle together those people he was involved with, he started to understand some quite important things about the way he related to them, which seemed to mirror how his father had related. I was able to point this out to him and from the picture on the page of his family tree, he began to think about how to reorganize his life and how he fitted into the family structure after his father had left that space.

People use different methods of drawing up a family tree but Figure 2.1 presents a few simple symbols that I find easy to use, and Figure 2.2 shows an example for you to see how they can be used in a diagrammatic format. I have given a written explanation of the family tree so that you can see the relationships illustrated.

Figure 2.1 Family tree – key symbols

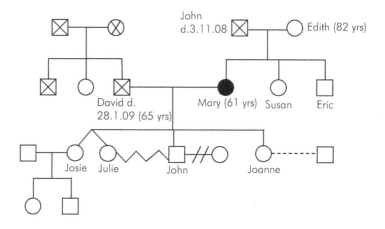

Explanation:

Mary is the client.

Mary's husband, David, died on 28 January, 2009. His parents are both deceased. He had an older brother who is also deceased, and a surviving sister.

Mary's father died shortly before her husband, and her mother is still experiencing her own grief.

Mary has a younger sister and brother. Mary has twin daughters, Josie and Julie, a son John and younger daughter Joanne. Josie is very busy with little children. Julie is not married and doesn't have a good relationship with her brother John who recently got divorced and has cut himself off from the family. Joanne lives away with her partner.

Figure 2.2 Example of a family tree

You might also want to encourage them to draw their family tree out on a large piece of paper for themselves afterwards, so that they can put family photographs in for each person. This is especially good as the tree can be handed down to grandchildren to talk about. In talking around the family tree, you can also talk about the place of the deceased in the family's life.

Literary activities: Writing poems, writing prayers, keeping journals, writing the 'unsent' letters and cards may help the client not only focus on the relationship but also put into words those things they have never expressed before. They can share them with you or not as they wish, but I have been encouraged by the way the writing and the sharing of such things has been cathartic and helpful for some of the clients I have seen. Something special goes on in the sharing, something that is treasured and held precious, and I think it validates and affirms the relationship in a new way.

During a session, I have sometimes given clients paper and pen and asked them to write about the deceased, or a letter to them, and I give them five or so minutes in which to do it. They invariably find they can start and then want to finish at home.

Dreams: Paint, draw or write out the dreams about the deceased. A few people would be able to do this quite easily but many will not. It might be easier for some to write them out. However, if you carry a box or bag with pastels and paper in, it could be quite a spontaneous thing to suggest. Because some people might get put off the idea as they were never any good at art at school, you might suggest they do symbols to represent what there was in the dream. The most important thing is to talk about the presence of the deceased that may have been felt. This will be looked at in more detail in Chapter 7.

Photographs: The idea of using photographs was discussed in the last chapter, so I simply add that as you look at the photographs also think about the relationships and the way people group themselves for them. Think about who is frequently next to whom and how they appear to be with each other.

Buttons and stones: Another way of finding out about relationships within the family when perhaps someone is not able to articulate too well, or the family is complex, is to use buttons or stones. It is easy to create a collection of different shaped and coloured buttons or stones over the years, but it may be easier to carry a small box of buttons about in your bag or a big coat pocket. You can use stones if you are generally in a room where you can have the stones in a basket or box. In any case I shall describe the activity as if for stones, though the same applies for buttons.

Ask the client to select a stone that would best represent themselves. You invite them to talk about why they chose that stone and what it is about the stone that is like them. You can make observations to help them, such as observing about the shape and form of the stone:

'I see there are a lot of sharp edges on the one side of this stone.'

Generally speaking they enter into the spirit of the activity and will start to see things in the stones that represent the characteristics of the people. For example, the client might have responded, 'I think my life has had lots of ups and downs so the sharp edges on this side look like the bad times I've been through.' It is important, however, not to interpret for your client, but merely make observations. You then ask them to select stones for other people in the family including the deceased. As they pick them and talk about them you get them to place them down on the table, or floor whichever is easier. It is then interesting to point out the way the client has placed the stones, because in many instances it can reveal the way the family is relating to each other.

IMPACT ON YOU AS A LISTENER

Reflect here on some of the struggles you might have experienced when listening to the client talk about their relationship with the deceased.

As you listen to the client's stories that describe their relationship, there is another relationship to be considered, that is the one you have with your client. Some of your struggles with the client might be reflecting the way other people struggle with this person. The struggles you have might also suggest to you why there might have been some difficulties in the relationship with the deceased. These struggles, it goes without saying, are the sort of thing that can be taken to supervision in order to gain another perspective and support, without shame and without blame. I used the bereavement team to help me with this and we found that there were some quite important things that we struggled with as we listened to accounts of people and their relationships, good and bad. So, here are some of our struggles. You might identify some of the ones you have experienced and, of course, you will have your own that might not be mentioned here.

It can be difficult not to judge. With the best will and training in the world, it is sometimes hard not to judge what you are hearing. When you are listening to another person's version of a relationship or a description of a person you may start to dislike them. Maybe the client and the deceased related to each other in ways you find difficult. (Other family members or friends in their lives might have found this difficult too, so it might be important to have it at the back of your mind as you try to sort it out for yourself in supervision.) Being empathic might prove difficult and if you are like me and every shade and cloud passes over your face, you have to exercise strict control over those facial expressions that might communicate disapproval. A raised eyebrow or a frown might just be enough to set up barriers. So while it is important to keep in mind that each relationship has its own validity, you probably need to talk it over with your supervisor so that you can diffuse your emotions before the next session, or unpick the reasons why the relationship or personality is causing you difficulty.

Another issue could be suspecting that we are not getting a true picture of the deceased. Helping people to become honest is not easy, especially when the old adage 'You mustn't speak ill of the dead' seems to be in operation. It is hard to know how far you can go in exploring relationships, especially when you suspect there may be difficult issues that could be lurking below the surface. Maybe it is a little cynical to say that no relationship is without its darker side, but some may be darker than others. We have to make sure we are not offending the client and at the same time we can only go with what they give us. It is up to them how much they share, and some may wish to maintain a protective shield around the relationship they had. That is the way it will be until, if ever, they wish to talk about something that may have been painful or difficult to handle.

If you find, however, that the client is sharing deep issues of abuse and violence you will need to talk about this in supervision as soon as you can, as you may be carrying dark images around with you for some time. It may be that this issue needs professional counselling and you will need to refer your client on to a counsellor, which may be difficult to do after they have opened up and shared with you. So you will need to refer back to your working agreement or contract, when you made it clear that if they needed expertise that you could not provide, you would suggest referring them to a counsellor.

It can be difficult to get a picture at all of the deceased. Sometimes the relationships you encounter are really complex, and trying to understand the different facets may be difficult. It will require a lot of your own energy to get the 'picture' of their relationship clear in your own mind. If you find that even after several visits this is still fuzzy, then there is something going on with the client, in the way they are telling you or not telling you about it. I suggest to the support workers that they can risk being direct and say:

> 'I don't seem to have a very clear picture of your husband in my head and some of the family relationships. I wonder if we can focus on him today and you can build a picture of him for me, so that I can get to know him better.'

Maybe it is hard for the client to talk about the deceased, and maybe you have to uncover that. It may be because they find it too upsetting to talk about the person and you have to go another route which might involve finding out about their family and their ways of coping before they can talk about the deceased in any detail.

Remembering what is said may be a problem. At first there seems to be an overload, a deluge of information and it is really important to get some of the details written down after the session as soon as you can. (Just to reiterate: we have a policy about keeping client details under lock and key at home with the details being shredded after the sessions are over. The brief session notes that outline what went on in each session are handed into the office after the sessions are concluded and kept for several years.) It also might be the way somebody is telling their story that makes it difficult for you to sort out what is going on and to remember it. Some people tell their story in such a way that you find it hard to stay interested, sad to say. So I guess something is happening there that needs to be talked about in supervision.

Some family dynamics may be difficult to accept because they are different to our experience or our values, and there might be some cultural issues that really cause us difficulties. You might find it hard to accept, for example, the way a woman has been treated and you might find yourself passing judgement on that family or practice. It might upset you so much that you miss some of the other issues that are around. As I told Ruth, in the Introduction (see page 20), she brings her whole self into the session, her life experiences and her prejudices. It is not wrong to find yourself struggling with another culture's practices, but you may have to own up to it and talk it through at supervision, as it might be a hindrance when working with that particular client. It would be good to get it off your chest too.

The client's circumstances might sometimes remind us of our own. What happens when you find that the situation you go into is very like your own and the relationship resonates with one of your own relationships? When this happens it can be difficult to remain detached from the client's story and be non-judgemental of the characters in that story. These are times for honesty in supervision; after all, you are there as a person too. Maybe by talking through the situation in supervision you can identify things for yourself and for your client. It is important for you to be able to separate out your story from theirs, so that you do not take up their story as your own.

Other areas of struggle are when the values of the person you are visiting are in conflict with your own, or there is a conflict with your own experience. There may also be times when what is being said sets off a reaction in you, perhaps tears, anger, anxiety or deep sadness. No doubt about it, there will be times like this. If you are a caring and compassionate person who wants to help others you will sometimes find yourself affected by what is said. If you find yourself with tears welling up, then be honest and say:

> 'I've been moved by what you've told me, and I can feel the tears coming, but my concern is for you. How are you feeling at this moment?'

These are all situations for a good session in supervision.

And, last but not least, one of the biggest traps we can fall into is not to leap in and rescue. It is hard to own up to the fact that we can be guilty of rescuing people; after all, aren't we only trying to help? The problem is that rescuing others is taking over and being in control and not allowing others to learn from their experience. What sort of things do I mean? They can be little things, like jumping in to defend someone when they can and should speak for themselves. Or there can be bigger issues like offering to do things for others when they should be doing them for themselves. If the client needs to contact someone they should be encouraged to do it for themselves. If they do not want to do it, you can help them think through what is creating the block, or think about ways round it, or what would be the consequences of not contacting. As a mark of respect for the client we need to allow them to fail if need be, because it is not our responsibility, it is theirs. You might want to help somebody get into groups or get started in a social activity, and in your eagerness and desire for the person to be taken care of and helped, you have gone to some lengths, like making phone calls, offering to give a lift, and so on. It is as well to learn early on in the helping profession and pastoral world not to take on somebody else's life and issues for them. They see it eventually as being taken over or being controlled. You will end up taking the blame for things when they go wrong, too.

In summary:

- Be careful not to direct people towards 'letting go' or breaking the bond with the loved one. From research findings we can say that many people's relationships continue after death and it is important to honour that continuing bond without suggesting that the ties be cut.

- Use the approach to encourage the client to explore their relationship and to gain meaning from it. Respect what they want to do with the relationship.

- Have an attitude that is curious about the deceased, their relationship, the relationships with others in the family, outside friends and work colleagues.

- In the case where the client is struggling with regret and other issues, significant support happens when you reflect what their struggle is and then explore the relationship with them.

- It is important to be honest about the way someone, or their story, or their relationship impacts you and to take that material to supervision, so that you can explore what is going on in the relationship you have with the client.

CHAPTER 3

Element 3: There is a life to celebrate

❀ There is a story
❀ There is a relationship
❀ **There is a life to celebrate**
❀ There is a legacy left behind
❀ There is a strategy for coping
❀ There is a journey undertaken

There seems to be a trend in society about the way we conduct or think about funerals, moving towards more of a celebration of the life of the loved one rather than having a sombre ritual. I am not sure how widespread it is, but certainly in my work with bereaved clients I am hearing more and more about the way they wanted to celebrate the life of the deceased. This is reflected in the number of funeral services that now have a theme of celebration and thanksgiving for the life that was lived, with variations in music played and eulogies given. At the outset of the grieving process, then, many people want to think positively about their loved one's life. They want to recall the great, good and funny things and think well of the life that has now come to an end. This may be a good thing for friends and colleagues and more distant family members, but it may not have such lasting impact for closer family. As time goes on, the missing of the loved one becomes more present and deeply felt, and the reality about what death actually means sets in as they begin to mourn and grieve. It is hard then to feel like celebrating and giving thanks.

So what do I mean by 'there is a life to celebrate' when we come to this element of the bereavement conversation? It certainly is not the first thing or even the second thing we would do in our bereavement sessions. However, as you have listened to stories and you have explored the relationships, it might be a natural element in your conversation as you turn to thinking about what was really good about the life of the deceased. It is a powerful thing to see how clients can light up with animation when you start to ask questions like, 'What would your husband have been proud of in his life?' It might not be that you mention the word 'celebrate' as that might not feel right for the client. But as you tease out the achievements and what is most remembered about the deceased, you are in fact celebrating their life.

Many bereaved people may regard their bereavement as something they have to endure; something has happened that they have no control over. In this element I am suggesting that we can help clients become more active in their grief. By looking at the life of the deceased in constructive ways they might be able to make some choices about how they view the life of their loved one, and their own life. I am here influenced by the writing of Robert Neimeyer who would regard grieving as 'something we do, not something that is done to us' (2000, p.91). So, rather than viewing the grieving process as a passive process of waiting, the client might be encouraged to regard it as a time of activity, sometimes involving mental and emotional activity as well as physical. Neimeyer also suggests that 'grieving is the act of affirming or reconstructing a personal world of meaning that has been challenged by loss' (p.92). The loss of a main character in the story of the client's life forces the bereaved person to come to terms with how the rest of the story will be written. It may mean an examination of all that has gone before and either affirming the previously held beliefs and foundations of their lives and strengthening them, or reconstructing the meaning of life and finding a new purpose. I would see that in examining the life of the deceased there may be ways of coming to some deeper understandings about what they might see as a way forward for themselves, perhaps in continuing something that a parent or partner has achieved or stood for.

At a time when people are at their most vulnerable in their grief it is as if they have to relearn how to live and how to be. Attig articulates it this way (2001, p.41):

> Relearning the world after someone we love has died is not a matter of taking in information or mastering ideas or theories. It is, rather, a matter of learning again *how to be and act in the world* without those we love by our sides.

This relearning of how to be and act may be closely connected with the life and personality of the deceased.

A young man I worked with began to celebrate who his father was and came to some life changing decisions about how he would live his own life in the future. He did not want to 'be' his father but he wanted to be 'like' his father and we were able to identify certain areas where he particularly wanted to do this. It would mean some changes but he started to understand more about who he was as he examined the life of his father.

It is, I believe, in the context of seeking strands of continuity in the relationship to the deceased (Neimeyer, 2001) that the concept of celebrating the life of the deceased fits. In celebrating the achievements, the character and the person, we are enabling the client to gain a perspective, some new understandings perhaps, about the life of the deceased so that a transition might take place. By bringing to mind the real life of the deceased and sharing in the spoken word with another, the actual significance of the life that was lived is allowed to take on true meaning.

It is perhaps timely to pause here and to think about the significance of our own lives, and what makes our lives meaningful. Reflect on what you would want others to celebrate about you and your life. Also reflect on what people who have been bereaved want to tell you about what their loved ones have done in their lives.

I have heard celebratory stories about the type of person that people liked and loved, for example, 'He was well thought of – a rock – and I was so amazed at how many people came to his funeral. They must've thought well of him, mustn't they?' People want to celebrate the kind of spouse the deceased was, with descriptions like 'faithful, loving, laughing, joking and generous.' They celebrate such things as the way the deceased was regarded by others in the community, and how involved they were perhaps in a society, club, or a place of worship. For example the father of a client I saw was one of the founding members of a rock climbing club to which the whole family belonged. It was eventually a place where the client could return to celebrate his father's contribution and efforts as well as a place to feel close to his father. There can be a celebration of how the deceased did a lot for others; how they supported those in need; and perhaps there might have been membership of social action groups or involvement in a local charity or a local hospital which deserves celebrating.

Achievements are always a pleasure to talk about and some can come as a surprise to you, as people tell you about the life of the deceased who might have had varied and unusual interests. Be prepared to be surprised by extraordinary things achieved by ordinary people. We have come across such interesting things as a couple who won awards for rock and roll dancing; a man who formed a jazz band and made recordings; someone who in a previous career played for some of the famous artists in the pop music world but who later lived a reclusive life so that no one really knew of his former glory. Some clients remember and celebrate that their loved one won achievements in sport, making their mark in local athletics, football, soccer or rugby clubs; and people are proud of business successes where hard work and long hours were rewarded by success. We should not overlook those whose loved ones have served in the armed forces; there are often medals given for gallantry or heroic deeds performed in armed combat to celebrate. Sometimes the collection of medals and awards is the poignant reminder of the person who earned them and wore them with pride.

It does not always have to be that people's achievements and successes in life have been recognized by other people. We can value someone simply for who they were in the family and in relationship with us. A wife might want to 'celebrate' her husband for the way he parented their children, and the practical skills that were so valued, like being a good gardener, or that he was a brilliant handyman. As you listen to these accounts of people, point out the depth of real appreciation that you hear being expressed, for example for the excellent jobs that were done around the house, the early morning cups of tea made even in the depths of winter which showed the care and consideration of a man for his partner. Maybe what was valued most was that she was a good housewife and her husband was proud of the relationships she made, appreciating how supportive, gentle and kind she was to him and the family.

Some will want to appreciate the way their loved one was an 'over-comer', how in life they had faced many difficulties and though they had not perhaps been highly educated, they were philosophical and perhaps had a committed faith that got them through many tough times. Maybe there have been deaths of children in the past and the parent who has recently died grieved for the rest of their life but in the grief still loved and reached out to the other children and other families in the community. Sometimes there have been extraordinary things achieved, charitable trusts formed and works that have come out of people's heartbreaking situations, and these things too are remembered with poignancy and pride.

Others will want to remember and honour the memory of how bravely their loved one went through the horrifying illness which was so awful for the family; but the way the deceased endured it left them amazed and asking, 'How could she have coped so well?' The inner strength and fortitude shown in the grips of pain and anguish gained the admiration of the family. Some want to celebrate that it was a good death, not because death is good, but because the deceased made it special in preparing the family for it and for what was to follow; perhaps in the way they planned it by writing letters or planning the funeral service ahead of time.

You hear so much about the deceased, it is really a privilege. But what you need to do is sort out the memories and the stories so as to assist your clients in celebrating.

HOW DO YOU CELEBRATE THE LIFE?

> Key Listening Activity: Identify the reasons for
> celebration and validate the significance of them.

In this conversation you are having with a bereaved client, there have been stories about the illness and the deceased's life, and there have been stories that reveal the relationships in their life, and then there are stories that signify who the person was and what their life was about. These latter stories are the ones we have to listen out for at this point, so that we can identify facets of the life to be celebrated. Your client will not be waving a flag saying, 'I'm now celebrating the life of my loved one.' They are just telling you a series of stories in response to your gentle probing. It is for you to identify the things that can be celebrated and to show them to your client so that they can begin to validate the significance of them.

Brenda and Barry had two little boys, but he died of cancer in his late twenties, after two years of being at home where Brenda nursed him while caring for their lively and active sons. She was suffering from exhaustion but she wanted to do what she could for her sons. The support worker asked Brenda this question, 'What would your husband have been proud of in his life?' It led to some deeper understanding of their relationship as well as what she could celebrate about him.

> *Brenda*: He kept racing pigeons in a loft at the bottom of the garden, and won a few cups at the club, which he was surprised about as he hadn't been doing it very long at the time. He enjoyed looking after them and talking to them. I thought they were quite smelly and they'd often leave dirty droppings on my clean washing, so they weren't my favourite. He liked them though and he'd go off early on a Saturday morning with a couple of them in the basket hoping to win.

> *Support worker*: He must have been very proud having won some cups, and it sounds as if he was quite gentle in caring for them. It was a special hobby for him and he must have found some like minded people at the racing club. How did they take to him coming in and winning some races?

The support worker selected from what Brenda had given him in trying to help her celebrate something about the interest Barry had with his pigeons. What the support worker did was to enter into the story of the successes Barry had, the enjoyment he got from the birds, as well as what it revealed about his character. The support worker had also used his imagination in thinking about how Barry had needed to be patient and gentle with the birds to help them settle and be content. By celebrating Barry's interest the support worker reframed Brenda's story, and used it to probe a little further about Barry's relationships with the other club members.

Brenda: I suppose they were a bit put out at first, but he was very friendly and he became quite popular with them. It was the same wherever he went, people really liked him, he had that way with him, you know – he never met a stranger.

Support worker: It sounds as if you admired the way he could make friends. And the way they were drawn to him sounds very special. He was quite a character by the sounds of things.

Brenda: Oh, you can say that again. He was the life and soul of the party and very generous natured. Give anyone what he had in his pocket if they needed it.

Support worker: You seem to be remembering that with some warmth. You can really appreciate that he was good natured and generous hearted and people liked him a lot.

In such a way we can work towards helping the client rethink the life of their loved one so they can start to think about the significance of the life and how it mattered to them and to others. The questions people often ask are, 'What was it for?' 'What was it all about?' 'What did it all matter in the end?' 'He's gone and nothing's left.' It is perhaps part of our humanity that we want our lives to be significant. We want to matter to someone else and perhaps to others, to be remembered for having an important place in our community and work places. I am not suggesting that we want to be celebrities, far from it, but there is something about being part of something bigger and being known for who we are and what we stand for. It could be quite significant in itself for the client to be able to answer some of those questions, even if they have not asked directly. That someone outside the family has recognized the worth of their loved one's life could be a way of changing the client's perspective. I hope I am not being presumptuous when I say I think most of us would want to live a successful life or a life of some worth.

So, perhaps at this point it might be profitable for you to pause and to consider what you think of when you think of a successful life.

I asked the bereavement team what they thought of when they thought of having lived a successful life. Here are some of their thoughts: they wanted to have gained an inner contentment in life; they valued their relationships with others in their lives; they hoped that they would be able to live as if their cup was always half full and be someone who could encourage others. They wanted to have provided for their families and to have been seen to have provided; they wanted to have successfully brought up well-adjusted children who were respectful and respected and who knew right from wrong and had good values; and some thought of it as providing an 'heir' to all they'd acquired, not only materially but emotionally and philosophically. That's quite a list, and I wonder how it compares with yours?

Now, how can thinking through what you consider to be a successful life help you work with your clients? I believe it can be at least informative, in that you have formulated some of your own ideas and as you listen to the lives of others it may help you form questions, for example:

> 'How did he look at life – was his cup always half full or half empty?' Or,

> 'What was important to her in life?' Or,

> 'What were some of his ideas of parenting your children?'

I must point out here that we are not trying to compare our own ideas with those we are listening to in order to judge them. We are using those ideas to inform our work in this element. We accept that others are different and we can help the client think constructively about their loved one's life and about their own. Maybe it is easier for those who are financially secure; not having to worry about material things, they can give thought to other aspects of their lives. This is a privileged place to be in life and many will perhaps have taken it for granted, while those who find it hard to cope with the material world will have a different priority. For instance, if your client's loved one has spent their lives trying to provide for their families, it would be helpful to acknowledge that working hard was important to them. Their priority in life was to earn enough money to be able to be comfortable and provide security for their family. That is worthy of celebration.

People will often say, 'He was just an ordinary man, he didn't do anything special.' I suppose it is in these instances that we can help them see the remarkable in the ordinary. Maybe some people lived lives on their own terms and the way they lived was not harmful to others. It could be possible to celebrate the independent nature of such a person;

they went their own way but they were happy about it. For other 'unremarkable' people's lives, even not striving, not being envious, not chasing after ambition, but living out their own convictions, can be celebrated and given value.

For the person who was difficult to handle, it might be possible to celebrate that they had been successful in overcoming their background and 'difficulties'. If we go back to Brenda and Barry, the support worker found out that Barry had been a real tearaway in his youth and had been a handful for his parents. You could say he had been a bit of a maverick, but at an early age he had set up in his own business as a plumber. He had channelled his considerable energies into a business and, because of the person he was, the business had done well so they had been able to move house. He had got plans for the future, for holidays and for expansion of the business, and then he was diagnosed with cancer. He had managed to get someone to look after the business while he was undergoing treatment, but he never did return to active work. The support worker was able to say to Brenda:

> 'From what you're telling me, Barry channelled his energies into setting up his own business and it seems that he was very successful. He'd really turned his life around, hadn't he?'

She was pleased to hear that from an outsider – someone who could help her see beyond the story into the essence of who Barry had been. She was able to go on to revisit the time around the illness and to remember how he had been strong even then, though it had felt like madness at times. It was as if she had been given permission, and had been freed up, to think of him in a more positive light, seeing how his strength of character had helped him cope in the awful times through the illness. She began to think about ways in which she could share some of those aspects of Barry with her boys and help them to be proud of their father.

What about those who do not want to celebrate the life, and can not remember anything good about the deceased? One of our clients had experienced a disappointing marriage:

> *Client*: My husband worked late and often used to come home so exhausted he'd fall asleep in the chair. I didn't appreciate that, I can tell you, and I would get on at him to get the jobs done. He used to

say it was his job to bring in the bread and butter, but I was working too, wasn't I?

Support worker. It sounds as if he really felt it was important to provide for you as a family. That seems to have been one of his values in life.

This started the client on a journey towards a new understanding of what had been important to her husband and she began to celebrate this as one of his positive characteristics. She was helped to see that he really did work hard and some other things came out that she was able to begin to value. Her husband had taken it as his parental role always to go to the children's parents' evenings at school, and to be at any events they were in, which were many as they were very talented on and off the sports field.

The support worker was able to say:

'It sounds as if he took his children's education seriously too. He'd made it a priority to be there for them and that was something special about him.'

The client became aware that she had not acknowledged how important their children's education had been to her husband and how in taking it seriously he had showed how much he was committed to his children. Because the support worker identified the husband's priorities and values and was able to validate them, the client began to be able to celebrate a little more the man her husband had been. Of course, this had its repercussions as she felt quite sad that she had nagged him and taken him for granted. It had not been a good marriage in her eyes, but she was left thinking about him and perhaps herself in a different way.

Sadly, there will also be those relationships that have been scarred by the behaviour of the deceased, someone who had been abusive, physically, verbally, emotionally or sexually. It is certainly hard to ask the client to celebrate this person's life because the impact on the client has been so negative. The truth, of course, is that few people are all bad or all good. People who have been continually abused can struggle with coming to terms with this, as it is more acceptable to them to think in black and white terms. Perhaps for years they had tried to protect the abuser and they had wanted to think of them in positive ways, but the abuse still continued. For us to ask them to think of the good things in this person's character seems like asking them to return to that place of being a victim. It might feel as if we are asking them to believe they were wrong and they brought the abuse on themselves. You may have to consider carefully whether you can go into this dimension or not with such a client, and some careful supervision will help you think this through before going ahead. It also may mean that this client needs to have more specialized counselling in the area of dealing with the abusive relationship.

In the main, however, it is possible to validate the life of the deceased through identifying the ways in which they lived their lives and made an impact in their world. This can be beneficial for the client and their family as it may set them on new paths of thinking about their own lives, as well as looking at the meaning and significance of their family, work, and belief systems. In getting to know details about the life of the deceased, and thinking about what they would have thought was important, we can start to guide the client into appreciating the uniqueness of their loved one. By doing this we can help them see the real value of the life their loved one lived, however long or short the life span. This can be done only by remembering, not by forgetting. People need to talk about their loved one so that they not only remember, but are able to find a new place eventually for those memories and emotions that are attached to the deceased. In asking good and searching questions you may be able to help the client reorganize their thoughts, memories and emotions, so that they can live more constructively with the pain of their loss.

WHAT QUESTIONS CAN YOU ASK?

As you look through the questions listed below, you will notice that some of them seem to be asking the same type of thing. This is because the way we phrase some questions will be more helpful to some than others, and some people respond differently to some phrasing. As you develop your experience in this particular element you will find out what works well, and these might help you think of your own when you are in your conversations with the client and you want to try to move the conversation into this element. I am not suggesting you use all of these questions, of course, but some of them may open up the way forward for helping the client think through how they can celebrate the life of their loved one.

What will be the thing you'll remember most about... (name)?

What would other people's view be of... (name)?

What would others remember about him?

What did... (name) think about his job? Would he have felt it was important in life?

What was... (name)'s relationship with your children? What did you think of her as a mother?

What were some of the things that she felt were important in life?

What makes you happy when you think of... (name)?

What would... (name) have been proud of in his life?

What would he have wanted to be remembered for?

What were some of the achievements that she was proud of?

What kindnesses (care, consideration etc.) did he show?

Tell me something nice about him.

What words would best describe how he lived his life? Give me some examples.

Also remember to reframe what they have said in the context they used, e.g.,

'Perhaps you might say that one of his achievements was that he was a good provider... (that he was loyal...faithful...steady...a stable influence...that you worked as a partnership).'

WHAT TECHNIQUES CAN YOU USE?

The techniques listed below have been described in previous chapters. Again I would want to stress that you do not have to use all of these 'tools' but some of them are really helpful in starting off the conversation and focusing on the achievements or celebrations of the life of the deceased.

Memory jars: You might want to help the client use this jar to celebrate achievements, whereas in other elements you can use the jar for other types of memories.

Photos and videos: The most celebrated moments of people's lives are often captured in photographs or on audio-visual tapes and CDs. Some examples might be: weddings; the birth of children; christenings or baptisms; school achievements; college or university graduations. These can be a rich source of discussion about the meaning and significance people have given to their lives and the priorities and values people have lived by.

IMPACT ON YOU AS A LISTENER

It is tiring listening well to other people's stories and listening out for what they are saying, trying to pick up on the clues. It takes time and practice to develop the skill and art of listening. But I do believe we can listen at different levels, and at this point it would be good to remember that you can listen out for your own gut feelings too. What do I mean by this? Every person we encounter leaves imprints on us (more of that in the next chapter) so, as we listen to the stories and descriptions about the deceased, we begin to get a 'feel' for the person. Of course, we have to check those out and so you can tentatively ask if your picture is right. Notice what is going on for you though, and ask yourself a few questions, such as:

> When you're listening to the way your client talks about their loved one, what are they telling you about this person who's a stranger to you? Do you feel you're getting to know this person?
>
> What are you learning about the way they lived their life?
>
> Would you have liked this person you're being introduced to? Why? Why not?
>
> Were some of their values the ones that you'd hold, or perhaps they're totally opposite to yours?

It is important to be honest with yourself, because if you are not you will not be able to give the client your honesty. For example, it may be that something about the deceased's actions seems hard for you to accept. In using your gut reaction you might feel more inclined to ask your client about their response, whereas you might have missed it if you had not been aware of your own reaction. It does not have to be a profound question, simply:

'How did you feel about that?' Or, 'How did you react to that?'

You can then go on to explore the impact on the client. If it has impacted you it might have had the same impact on the client and they were afraid to admit it or to voice it.

It is such a relief to take these issues to supervision, because it is not possible to like everybody and appreciate the good in everyone. There may be frustrations you need to voice and explore; you may need to deal with something in your own past that comes up; or you may need to work through how somebody reminds you of someone in your own life. You may also need help in identifying what there is in the deceased's life to celebrate. Or you may need support in discussing a referral for further counselling with a client who is in need of qualified help in an area such as abuse. It is better to explore those in an open way than have them block the work you do with your client.

In summary:

- We are enabling the client to gain a perspective, some new understandings perhaps, about the life of the deceased when we can celebrate their achievements, the character and the person.

- The listening activity is to identify the reasons for celebration and validate the significance of them.

- We can help our clients see the remarkable in the ordinary.

- Also remember to try to reframe what they have said in the context they used.

CHAPTER 4

Element 4: There is a legacy left behind

- ❀ There is a story
- ❀ There is a relationship
- ❀ There is a life to celebrate
- ❀ **There is a legacy left behind**
- ❀ There is a strategy for coping
- ❀ There is a journey undertaken

What do you think of when you hear the word legacy? Wills? Solicitors? Inheritance? Money? I guess we do naturally think of those things, especially linked to bereavement. But I wonder if we can think a little beyond the practical, legal domain and think in terms of people and what they pass down to us, apart from the family portraits and jewels. When I was leaving America after completing my five years of study, I was given a little plaque as a gift, one of those that come with a wise saying done in ornate calligraphy. Friends of mine had given me this: 'Some people come into our lives, make footprints on our hearts and we are never the same.' I think I made a joke of it then, being a little embarrassed, but I have often wondered about it and the truth of those words. I wonder what the impact of my life was on them; I never did ask. Maybe one day I will.

When we talk with bereaved people and we have heard their stories, we have explored their relationships, and validated the lives of the deceased we can try to discover the legacies left behind for the one grieving. One of my experienced bereavement support workers says that when she dies, she wants everyone to cry. She wants them to miss her; she wants to know that her life has been worthwhile. Am I presuming by thinking that we all want to be significant to others? I know I do, but I also want to leave something of me behind. A psalmist in the Old Testament writes, 'As for man, his days are like grass, he flourishes like a flower of the field; the wind blows over it and it is gone, and its place remembers it no more' (Psalm 103: 15-16; New York International Bible Society 1978, p.564).

I don't know about you, but I want to be remembered at least by those who've loved me, and I want my story and my personality to be passed on to others in the family. I want my nephews and nieces to say, 'Do you remember Auntie Dodie. She would...?' Maybe that's all I can expect? A friend often talks of his father who had worked hard all his life as a headmaster of one of those small privately owned schools that were popular in England after the Second World War. His father's life went into making it a success; there were many sacrifices made along the way and many setbacks too. None of his children wanted the legacy of the school, it didn't fit into their lives, and so it passed over to a Trust. What remains of his father's life work is a building named after him in a school that still exists today. Though as I listen to my friend, there is more than a building that remains of his father – as an individual his personal legacies have been considerable.

Personal legacies are important – those special things, the sayings, the memories, the gestures and the facial expressions that live on in our hearts and minds, in our children and grandchildren. Maybe the wind does blow over the place of the dead. But what can we do to reclaim the memory of, and give significance to, lives that have often been hard and yet have been important? We can talk about the important things in the life of the loved one. We can help the client think about the legacies, the lasting things that will be recalled. Robert Neimeyer has done some work on the concept of legacies which originates from his thinking that:

> Without really intending it, from our first days of life we appropriate ways of gesturing, thinking, speaking, feeling, and acting from our parents, relatives, friends, and even public figures with whom we identify. In a sense, then, we become living memorials to these persons, even after they themselves have died. (2000, p.149)

Thomas Attig (2001) talks about holding those we love in our souls; our souls have been touched so that our everyday lives are inhabited by those we loved. The reason we should spend time exploring legacies is encapsulated in what Attig has to say about them (p.49):

> Their soulful legacies include the roots of our individual, family, and community traditions, histories, and characters. They have shown and taught us ways of caring about, and loving, things, places, food, music, ourselves, others, and our families and communities.
>
> We give them places in the lives of our souls as we grow in understanding and appreciation of our roots in them. And we do so as we make ourselves at home again among things, places, food, and music, within traditions and with the friends, families, and communities they have touched…We make meaning when we deliberately cultivate traditions or soulful ways that we had abandoned, neglected, or failed to appreciate while they were alive and sense abiding connection to those who died as we do.

You will again see the direct influence of Neimeyer and Attig in this approach. I am indebted to them particularly for this element and how they have opened it up as a way into deeper places in the bereavement conversation.

Pause now and think about what sort of things you might want to hand down to your loved ones as a legacy. Would it be that special piece of china you have always cherished and you know that your granddaughter will love it in the same way? Would it be the love of carpentry and being able to shape wonderful and practical things out of wood? Would it be your love of books and words? Would it be the way you smile or your laughter? Would it be your patience or your common sense in a time of stress? Think also about what you have received from those in your family who have been before you. What have you gained from them?

Legacies can be wonderful things to have but they can also bring some difficulties. I will share some of the legacies we have encountered and some of the problems these brought too. One of our bereavement team went to see a woman whose husband had died and in the telling of the story it soon became apparent that her husband had wanted her to do something specific, and she was eager to do it, but anxious in case it could not be done. Her husband had begun to make a fort with soldiers and cannons. Unfortunately he had died before it was completed. She and her friends had agonized over what to do with this because her husband had wanted her to donate it to the local children's hospice. The friends completed the project and the splendid fort, now inhabited by infantry men and cavalry as well as Red Indians, was given to the children. They have been the grateful recipients of the legacy left behind by a thoughtful, caring and creative man. His wife was pleased to be able to fulfil his wishes, and proud of a man whose skills and care were going to live on by giving hours of pleasure to dying children.

A personal legacy can be what has been created in the home. Some of those things can be really helpful to recall and live with: the new kitchen that was designed and lovingly built; the fireplace that was constructed out of small briquettes; the garden that was lovingly tended; the bookshelves that still remain on a slant supported by a house brick. These are often a mixed blessing; they bring pleasure and pain. Everyday they can speak of the loved one but also emphasize the pain and loss. While on the one hand they can bring delight, on the other they represent a tie to the house or the garden. How difficult it can prove to be to move house, to leave behind things created with so much care that remind you of your loved one. Or if another relationship is entered into, what was left behind can cause distress. A mixed bag of emotions and concerns are wrapped up in legacies.

The husband who had big schemes and dreams for the house, but who never did complete his projects, leaves walls still to be plastered, doors still to be hung, and carpets still to be laid. The legacy his family struggles with is getting it all completed. Some people, however, relish accomplishing things that were dreamed of between the two of them. 'I'm getting it done – for him.' 'She would have wanted me to get on and do it; she always wanted the new bathroom.' For a season, the desires and wishes of the loved one can be the driving force behind some people's activities in creating changes in their homes and lives. Sometimes the question is:

> 'What follows after you've finished this project? How do you think you will feel then?'

This may extend also to holidays planned for and places to visit which are linked to the expressed wishes, or requests, of the deceased. The role of the support worker here is to help the client think through the impact the holiday will have on them, what will be good and what will be difficult. I worked with a young woman whose mother had died and had wanted her ashes scattered at her favorite holiday resort. How was I going to be helpful in this instance? I used some of my own concerns to help my client think through what it was going to be like taking the ashes aboard the plane and sitting with them on the flight.

> 'How will you carry them?' 'Where will you put them?' (Under the seat? In the overhead locker?)

We thought about what it would be like when they arrived and about finding the right place and the right time of day; we thought about how it would affect the holiday, at which point to scatter the ashes so the holiday would be of benefit to them all. With careful questioning, I helped her think about what she expected to get from it and what different members of the family might want and how they all might behave and why. Because I had put myself alongside her I was able to ask some pertinent questions, not being afraid to go into the details. I do not think it would have proved overly helpful just to say, 'So you're going to scatter the ashes in your mother's favorite spot.' This would have been a good start, but I needed to go on and discuss with her where that spot was going to be, how they were going to get there, and so on.

Animals can also be legacies, around which there can be several emotions. Perhaps in the instance where the cat or dog was always known as the deceased's, it can become a substitute object of affection, as if it were a direct link with the deceased. The animal can be a source of comfort for the family, or it can be a painful reminder of the loss. Sometimes when the animal has to be put down through old age, or illness or accident, the emotional outpouring can seem excessive until you know how the animal has represented the deceased person to the grieving family or person.

The legacy of a garden too can become a focus of special attention. Either the garden is tended and taken care of in memory of the loved one, which can be of positive benefit to the bereaved person, or it can become a real problem. The problem with the garden is in actually keeping the things that were planted alive, and each time there is a 'death' in the garden, the 'guilty' one feels the pain of letting the loved one down. There is also the growing practice where some people bury the remains of their loved one in their own gardens, so that a private 'memorial garden' has been created. This can cause friction in families, but also a long lasting tie with the property until it is sold or the person moves on. Digging up remains to move them on can dig up old memories and open old wounds. If you are listening to someone who has created a memorial garden, it could be helpful to ask several things:

'What plans have you got for the future of the house?'

'What might it be like to move and have to dig his ashes up?'

'What might it be like for other members of the family to deal with?'

'How have other members of the family responded to your garden memorial?'

Do not be afraid to enter into this discussion; we have known many people who have been helped to talk through the practicalities, or the difficulties, around their garden memorial.

Sometimes other people are the legacy and the bereaved person is expected to look after the family. Some deathbed requests or emotional legacies can be burdensome and feel like emotional blackmail after time, emotionally trapping the bereaved person. A young man whose father whispers to him, 'Make sure your mum and the kids are OK' feels the weight of responsibility for the rest of his days, or tremendously guilty when he fails. The wife who does not feel she has the freedom to have another relationship because she knew her husband would not have wanted her to 'replace' him. The young man who has been told by his dying father, or well-meaning relatives, that he is now 'the man of the house' can not live up to that responsibility when his mother enters into a new relationship. He has to renegotiate his place. He may struggle to come to terms with what he might see as betrayal of his father's love and a loss of his own status in the eyes of his family. Asking what the deceased person would have wanted will help you find out if there is an emotional legacy left behind, but it does not solve the situation for the bereaved person. So working out how the bereaved person can live with new circumstances requires patient and collaborative dialogue.

Not all legacies prove to be problematic, though. Sometimes it is helpful for the bereaved client to look for the genetic similarities – the face, the eyes, the nose, the mouth, the colour of the hair in the family. It is the same with beliefs and concepts that are passed on, that can be named and owned for their originator. It could be that there is a grandchild who comes out with the same kind of humour or the same laughter, and is a joy and comfort. Often families will want to perpetuate the memory of a parent or grandparent by continuing the familiar things she said and did.

There are also some practical things that get passed on, for example the wife who has kept the yearly calendar with all the birthdays on and the Christmas card list with addresses, so that eventually the husband can pick up the threads and restart the ritual if he wishes to. Then there was the wife who left a freezer full of prepared meals for her husband, which of course eventually needed restocking. By then he felt able to take on the responsibility of looking after himself. The question was asked, 'What was her wish for you in this, do you think?' It got him thinking about what she had planned for him and how she had taken control of various things in their life, not perhaps always to their mutual benefit. He held onto one meal that she had cooked and did not eat it; it was a reminder of her care and her love for him.

Many people have kept that 'special chair' in the living room and will not allow anyone to sit in it. Just a pointer here for you; if you see a person in their own home, it is advisable in the first session to ask where they would like you to sit, so you do not make an immediate blunder. They might be aware of the 'invisible presence', and this might give you the opportunity to explore their spiritual understanding and the significance of the 'presence' for them in a later session.

Some people will have collections that they have inherited: tapes, CDs, the music collection, the book collection, the video and DVD collections. People will play, read or watch them, or not; but they frequently find it difficult to dispose of them. One client made an astute observation about trying to give away some of her husband's music collection, 'Not many people want to take something that belonged to a dead person.' Some people will have 'collected' places and walks and are able to revisit the places and go on those favourite walks they shared together, and while it brings pain there is a modicum of comfort too for them.

As you can see, legacies come in all shapes and sizes and different guises, and I hope it has been helpful to think about the kind of thing you are looking for, so that you can identify it with the client. Why is it important to talk about the legacy or legacies that someone leaves behind? I believe it is part of helping the client understand the meaning to the life that was lived, long or short. The life of their loved one was of worth. The love they have for their child, (their father, mother, husband, wife, partner, lover, or friend) is part of their own life story and has a place that is significant in its impact on them and their future. What has been left behind? What has been passed on or down? What imprint or footprint has been made on their heart by the loved one? Attig (2001) writes about making a way for lasting love for the deceased in this way: 'Our appreciation of them can grow indefinitely. They were and remain unique and irreplaceable' (p.51).

WHAT DO YOU DO WITH THE LEGACY?

> Key Listening Activity: Discover it to
> encourage them in giving worth to the life.

Within the stories you hear, there are nuggets of gold to be mined, to be brought to the surface and to be discovered for their own worth. That is how I view looking for the legacies that have been left behind. I have never been gold mining; the nearest I came to it was in South Africa when visiting Pilgrim's Rest, now a museum village depicting the life of the panhandlers and miners who lived there in the days of the gold rush. One thing I know is that you would be careful about looking for gold while sifting through the gravel and dirt in the rivers and streams, and you would have to have a trained eye looking for what might glitter in the sun. In the same way we need to be watching out for those nuggets of legacies that can be discovered and talked about until they shine, or can be put aside until the client feels ready to deal with them.

Like the previous element where we were celebrating the life, I would not go into this element too soon. It has its own timing, perhaps when people are more open to thinking about their loved one in a more objective way. We should probably be aware that there may be things left behind that need to be dealt with, that do not immediately surface when the pain of loss and sorrow are shouting to be heard.

In discovering the legacy you will be encouraging them to give worth to the life of their loved one. A support worker saw a client who was still grieving over the way his father died, unexpectedly in the client's arms. After several sessions the support worker invited her client to describe his father for her and through the way he talked about his father came the picture of a man of quiet resolve and integrity, whose appreciation for hard work and education was important to him as he raised his family in a new country. The support worker pointed this out to her client and he began to think about the way they had worked hard and had used the opportunities of the education system to better themselves. The support worker again pointed out that this was part of his father's legacy to them all. The client thanked her for giving him a view of his father that had made him proud as a son. The support worker had given value and worth to the father's life.

You might find that initially you will need to introduce the topic, until you are more practised in spotting the glints of gold. So it might be worth thinking of something to introduce it with; I usually try something along the lines of:

> 'I wonder if we can talk a little about legacies. Legacies are usually about the material things someone leaves for other people, like the family portraits, or the old Victorian sideboard. But, I wonder if we can begin to think a little about what… (name) has left behind for you. Not about what he has left for you in the house or the will, but what he has left of himself in your family.'

This can be a bit of a slow starter so it might be necessary for you to encourage them in it at first, though I have used it with young people and they are very quick to grasp the idea and run with it, especially if they are like their parent or grandparent.

WHAT QUESTIONS CAN YOU ASK?

Most of the time you would be listening out for the clues that reveal the legacy you can identify for the client from the stories or accounts they are giving you. But there will be times when you can ask more direct questions that can lead them to the discovery of the legacies for them-selves. Here are a few suggestions that you might try. Again, it might be better not to bombard the client with all of them, but a few well-chosen ones at the right time might prove fruitful.

> What sayings or mannerisms do you remember she had?
>
> In what ways are these reflected in your family life?
>
> What words of wisdom would she have for you now? What would she have wanted you to do… (in a given situation)?
>
> What things remind you of… (name), e.g. music, films, books, going out on walks?
>
> Who in the family is most like him?
>
> How do you see your husband reflected in the family?
>
> What would you say was his lasting legacy to you and the family?
>
> What can you see that he has left behind for you to enjoy?
>
> What philosophy (or way of thinking) do you think she has passed on to her family?

WHAT TECHNIQUES CAN YOU USE?

Family legacies: Ask them to work on a list of what they would like to pass on to their children or grandchildren. Get them to think of what might already have been passed on by the deceased.

Personal legacy: This activity is inspired by the imprint exercise by Robert Neimeyer (2000, pp.149, 150) and can be given to the client to do in their own time or you can use it in your session to help them focus. If they don't want to write it out then they can just talk to you about it. This works really well with adult children, after the loss of their parent, and it can work well with teenagers who have lost a parent or grandparent.

> The person who has given me the legacy is:
> I have been influenced by… (name) in some of the following ways:
>
> My values and beliefs: …
>
> The way I… (e.g., speak, smile, laugh):

The interests I have in: ...

My personality – especially the way I am: ...

Other things that I have learned from... (name) are: ...

Shared places and interests: Ask them to write about the shared places and interests and what the deceased would say and do in those places.

Taking on 'the mantle': This is the concept of having been given the legacy that has been passed on through a personality type or a particular characteristic.

Explain what the mantle is – e.g. the mantle was a cloak passed down in olden times from father to son or from king to prince or from prophet to prophet, so that the work or responsibility was carried on. You can then ask this type of question:

What is the mantle you think you have been given?

What does it feel like to have that mantle?

What will you do with it, now you feel it's been given to you?

Would you like to change it any way?

Would you like to pass it on to someone else so they can benefit too?

IMPACT ON YOU AS A LISTENER

You might find this more difficult to talk about at first as it feels like new territory, maybe an unusual topic for conversation. Perhaps it is possible to say that we do not tend to be overly thoughtful or analytical about the lives or impact of our loved ones until we focus on them, and not on ourselves. So, as you enter this element you might find that you and your client are stumbling around a little for some clear direction. They might not initially understand what it is you want them to think about, and that might make you feel uncertain. But persevere and you will find that this is really interesting and adds to the depth of their appreciation for what their loved one has left behind.

You might also find yourself a little emotional as they talk about their loved ones in this way, as it might touch chords in your own life and spark off remembrances of your own loved ones and what they have passed on to you and your family. Make a mental note of what goes on for you and either take it to your supervisor or think it through with someone close to you in your family (without of course divulging what has sparked it off for you).

You can never tell what is going to touch your own life. A client I saw about the loss of his father talked about the legacy of his father's model railway collection and how he loved to go to the shed with his dad and watch him carefully paint and restore the old originals he had bought at auctions or fairs. They used to go together and spend time talking to other collectors and experts. Together they had made a whole model town and landscape for these trains to travel in. His love of the collection and the whole world of model railways was kept alive in honour of his father. What I was caught out by, however, was the emotional impact it had on me as I held the picture of him with his father, and I found myself feeling envious. My own father had died when I was nine and I would have loved to have shared with my father something of the experience this young man had shared with his. Not that I begrudged it him. But I found myself yearning again, even after all these years, for that bond and that type of connection I had longed for with my father.

So, you see, you can never tell when something is going to affect you. Be prepared to acknowledge the impact some of your clients' legacies can have on you, and be prepared to feel it and explore it when it is safe and right to do so.

In summary:

- We start our lives by imitating and taking on gestures, thoughts, ways of speaking, feeling and acting from family and friends and others we come into contact with or whom we admire from afar.

- We can talk about the things that were important in the life of the loved one and help the client discover the legacies, the lasting things that will be remembered and passed on.

- In discovering the legacy you will be encouraging the client to give worth to the life of their loved one.

- Think with your client what imprint or footprint has been made on their heart by the loved one.

CHAPTER 5

Element 5: There is a strategy for coping

⊛ There is a story

⊛ There is a relationship

⊛ There is a life to celebrate

⊛ There is a legacy left behind

⊛ **There is a strategy for coping**

⊛ There is a journey undertaken

Do you have a particular strategy for coping when life gets difficult? Giving this some thought, I realize that I am a list maker. I sit down and think of all the things I have got to do about a situation and when I need to do them, and then put them in the diary, as I have learnt that if I leave them on the paper (or back of the envelope) as a list, nothing will happen – except that I will lose the list. When things get really emotionally difficult for me, I realize that I tend to retreat into myself more than I would normally, and spend time with my own thoughts and worries. I have to be drawn out of them by some careful questioning, usually by a close friend or my husband. This is unusual because I am quite a talker ordinarily. So what does that say about how I cope? Years ago I would have said that my preferred way of coping would be to talk it out. Now I realize that strategy does not always apply.

When my mother died, I recognized that I kicked into this practical approach. Sitting by the side of her bed while she was 'sleeping' I had spent time writing out some of the details of her life for the minister who would be taking the funeral service. I started organizing the funeral in a methodical way with all the information to hand and making lists of the process to go through and who to contact and when. I did not dwell on the loss of my mother until after the funeral had passed and I was exhausted. As three sisters we had gone through a vigil, waiting and watching. Only afterwards did I begin to feel the impact in my body. I am not sure even now that I have allowed myself to feel the full emotional loss. That has given me an interesting insight into the way some people I talk with may be handling their grief.

Perhaps we have assumed that people need to cry and to mourn in a particular way. Perhaps also we have thought that men and women grieve differently. My own experience of how others present with their grief and my own recent experience has made me question what does go on for us. I have been interested in the work of Martin and Doka (1999) who suggest there are several healthy ways of coping with grief rather than stereotyping men and women into gender specific responses. They describe three specific patterns: an 'intuitive pattern', an 'instrumental pattern', and a 'blended pattern'. The *'intuitive pattern'* is one in which the individual expresses and experiences grief in an overtly emotional way. People who operate in this pattern tend to share their inner experiences. The *'instrumental pattern'* is one in which the individual expresses and experiences grief in a physical or cognitive way. A *'blended pattern'* represents a certain amount of coping and moderate levels of emotional intensity but there will be a dominant instrumental or intuitive pattern prevailing. Judging by this description, I realized I responded much more in an 'instrumental' way than I thought I would. This has surprised me greatly as I imagined I would have been much more 'intuitive'; after all, I'm the one who cries in the trailers and adverts at the cinema!

The aim of working with people is not to direct them towards a blended response, as if it were the most appropriate. People should be assisted to identify how they cope and to think about how each pattern has its strengths and its weaknesses. It is also suggested that these patterns of grief exist on a continuum. Bereaved people may respond to different losses in a different style; however, most bereaved people are consistent in their style. As the individual grieves, they would be most helped by working with their preferred pattern, and helped to look at the other ways of responding if their preferred pattern is not working for them.

This insight into grief patterns may explain for us how families are often at odds with each other as they grieve, not understanding how members of the family differ in the way they approach their grief. It is also possible that we might be making a mistake in unconsciously generalizing about the way men and women grieve. You will be able to identify the intuitive pattern of coping because the client will be open to talking about feelings, emotions, and their inner world. We make a mistake if we think this is only for women. Many men I have worked with have been able to articulate and have wanted to talk about their emotions and the inner struggles they have.

When you meet with someone operating in the instrumental pattern you will hear much more about their thoughts and actions, centred on plans, activities, wanting to find out and know. We again make a mistake if we think this is solely a man's domain. I have encountered many women who do not respond well to talking about their feelings; and some who have been eager to get to know as much as they could about the disease or cancer that their loved one died of, as a way to helping them come to terms with what they saw and experienced. An example of this is the woman who would only accept support because she had two children to bring up and saw their needs as paramount. So she would have support for them, talking about how the children were doing and how she was coping with them, but in the middle of it she would shed tears for her own loss.

How do you cope at times of stress and difficulty? Pause to reflect on some of your coping strategies, and perhaps ask someone who knows you well to comment on how they see you cope in difficult times.

Bereavement is perhaps one of the most difficult times in life we have to face, along with ill health and financial ruin, and even at the heart of these circumstances there are loss issues involved. The concept of grief patterns is useful and helps us identify those who will not respond well to talking about their feelings and those who will. In addition to thinking about grief patterns I have also identified certain practical strategies that people use to manage their grief. There are some ways that are fairly typical and some that are not. Some strategies and ways of coping are helpful and assist the bereaved person in coming to terms with their loss and making adjustments to their new life circumstances. There are other strategies, however, that can be less constructive in supporting the life changes that are needed. Let's take a look at some of the ways of coping and strategies we have come across.

The 'protective' strategy. There are some bereaved people who decide that their way of coping will be to be selective about who they will share with. Perhaps they will allow themselves into their feelings, usually (but not exclusively) only when their bereavement support worker is present because it feels safe. Of course, there may be other people they talk to, but often they will say that they can not go into their grief with others, especially their family and relatives because it is too painful for them all. Family members are often afraid of seeing each other cry and can not cope with their own emotions so they block them off from each other. The problem with this protective strategy is that no one knows how anyone else is doing and they can only imagine how each other is handling it. Sometimes they come to the wrong conclusions about each other. We have known mothers who have been quite agitated and even furious with their adult children because the children seem to be getting on with life and do not seem to be sad or affected in the way they are. I would suggest that as a support worker you start to question how others in their family are grieving only after you have established a good relationship with your client. You should ensure that they really sense you have been alongside them in their grief. Only a tentative question can be brought into this picture:

> 'How would you think your children might be experiencing their grief?'

I would also use something visual such as the 'Blob Tree' diagram (see Figure 5.1, page 141) and you can read the section on techniques for a way of using this diagram.

There are times when there is a real reason for not sharing, and for using this protective strategy for good purpose. After a tragic death or a suicide, some may want to pour it all out and talk it out (they will operate in an intuitive pattern). Some, however, may only want to talk with members of the family or those closely involved, as they can not face going over the details with other people. They may feel too vulnerable, and because they have not been able to come to an understanding of it they can not share the details with others outside the inner circle. I have addressed this in Chapter 1, but to reiterate, in the instances of tragic death or suicide, it would be wise to ask how much your client wants to talk about the death, and events leading up to it, and how much they want to explore what happened. It would be respectful not to push or pry, despite your own curiosity and need to know.

The 'keeping busy' strategy: There are those who adopt this strategy knowing that they do not want to stop and think about things, because they think it will be too emotional and they will not be able to cope. One man said that if he stopped, he was afraid he would be taken away. He was afraid of letting go to the point of 'cracking up' (his words) and not being able to function. People using this strategy will be blocking their thoughts and feelings by doing many other things, like the decorating, the gardening or cleaning the curtains and carpets. It is not always a negative strategy, either. There are times when it is an acceptable way of coping. We would say this was following an instrumental pattern. Some will need to put space between the event of the death and themselves, before they can go back to it and start to deal with it. Some of course, will appreciate the feeling of satisfaction that comes with activity. After the dark time of being immersed in the illness, or in the nightmare of a sudden death, they are starting to see some daylight and appreciate getting things done. Some will, as I have discussed before, have kept busy in order to fulfil the project that was planned by them as a family or as a couple. This is part of their memorial to their loved one.

The 'getting fit' strategy: There are those activities that are beneficial for the bereaved person. No one is going to stop someone from taking up exercise, walking, swimming, going to the gym – any activity that gets the body fitter and the mind clearer is to be encouraged. What we sometimes see in the bereaved person who does take an activity up is that it can become compulsive and obsessive. Frank was a fit man before Ann died, slightly overweight but healthy. He started going to the gym and as he told his support worker, 'I took it out on the tread mill. I pounded my pain away.' For a time he visited the gym for hours, punishing his body but feeling the relief of exhaustion afterwards. He lost weight and toned up but looked like a haunted man. His family were concerned and he knew he was distancing himself from them. It was only when he had 'burnt it all out' – to use his expression – that he found a place of peace.

Engaging in an extreme form of activity worked for him, as part of his instrumental pattern. Someone else, whose husband died in his late forties, decided to take up running, joining a club and progressing to marathon running for charity. Again she demonstrated her tendency towards the instrumental pattern. She became a dedicated runner and eventually started a new relationship with someone from the same club.

The 'fund raising' strategy: There are other activities that people sometimes get involved with in order to give themselves purpose. Some people go on the fund raising trail and become semi-professional charity campaigners. I would think that there are many hospices and research charities that have been well served by such people. Their dedication and commitment is outstanding. The driving force behind the work can be to give something back on behalf of their loved one so that the death would not have been in vain. We would not want them to stop their efforts. But we would not want them to have to carry on beyond the call of duty. Sometimes families can get caught up in the fund raising and lose sight of their own journey and the life of adjustment ahead of them. If some others in the family no longer want to take part in a fund raising event, there may be a real family crisis. There may be hurtful accusations made, such as, 'You don't care about him any more.' Again it is important to validate the client's own desire and goals, but at the same time encourage them to think through what might be going on for others in the family. Perhaps ask:

> 'What would it be like for you to give up the fund raising efforts?' Or,

> 'Let's think about how it might be for others in your family who are perhaps not dealing with their grief in the same way as you are.'

Or, if your client is the one who wants to give up on the fund raising:

> 'I guess you might be feeling a mixture of emotions about this. I wonder if you want to have a look at this with me, as other people in the family may be feeling quite differently to the way you are.

The 'taking care of others' strategy: Some will keep focused on looking after others. There are those whose role in life has always been to look after others; they are natural carers. After a death there may be family members who think that the bereaved wife or grandmother will be free to help out. It can be a bag of mixed motivations: some will become 'martyrs', or act out 'Cinderella Syndrome', enjoying feeling sorry for themselves because there is no one else to care. Some will bask in the thanks and praise of others. But mostly there will simply be a desire to help out and look after others – with some pressure from the family. This can be the case especially if they have spent time looking after their ill relative, and after the death there is a void. There is a vacuum where there was once a purpose in their life; it has been taken from them. They will perhaps turn to looking after elderly parents or young grandchildren, or perhaps their own children become the focus. They need to be fulfilling a role that gives life some structure and purpose for getting up and out of bed. This can be a successful strategy too, as the new focus can be helpful. However, a concern might be that they suppress their own emotions which in turn might make them tired, weary and perhaps depressed later. Just a gentle show of concern might be enough to get them to think about this:

> 'I wonder if you're much better at taking care of others than you are of yourself?'

This will undoubtedly bring about agreement, and so you can follow up by asking how they can take care of themselves and what it would look like for them to do that. Maybe they simply have not thought about it in this way. It may be necessary to suggest to them that they have an option to opt out of the caring role if they need to, as they are handling their own grief. This might be a time where the instrumental pattern has to be balanced out by taking care of the intuitive.

The 'isolation and withdrawal' strategy: A strategy that might get missed for a while is that of isolating oneself from friends and family. The bereaved person withdraws from life and from engaging with others. In some cultures withdrawal from the world happens as part of the bereavement ritual and it goes on in the family unit; for example, some eastern cultures will accept visitors to the house for a time to sit with the bereaved family. This is different from the withdrawal that isolates the bereaved person even from their family. For a time the family members understand that their parent does not want to do things like come for lunch or go out, but after a while they can realize that there is a pattern being established. The extreme loneliness of bereavement some experience can be heightened by the choice not to engage with others. I

once gently addressed this with someone who was habitually refusing
the invitations of her son and daughter, after she told me she felt they
were constantly 'on at her' about not coming to be with them. I said:

> 'Your loss has really affected your life and you're never going to be
> the same as you were. But I wonder if I might venture to say that it
> also feels really sad for your family, as they seem to be experiencing
> the loss of you too during this time.'

It is a fine line that people walk when they do not want to be involved in
family occasions, and who could blame them. It is hard for them to be
present at family gatherings when they are in much emotional pain, so it
is important for them to know when to stay away for their own good.
However, at the same time their families feel deprived of their presence
and their contribution to family life.

I have marvelled at the strength of the mother who courageously
faced the wedding of a daughter a few months after the loss of a
husband, both mother and daughter feeling joy and intense pain on a
day of celebration. It is hard to put a brave face on when others around
you are making merry and your heart is breaking with loss. It would be
important for the bereaved wife to take care of herself, while at the same
time remembering not to deprive her children and grandchildren of her
presence.

A support worker was working with a bereaved woman whose
husband used to go to the school football matches to watch their son
play. Her son was obviously feeling the loss of his father particularly at
these times. The client could not countenance going even when her son
asked her to go to watch him. The support worker said something gentle
like this:

> 'Your son really misses your husband's presence with him at these
> matches. It sounds as if he might have a desire to maintain the rela-
> tionship he had with your husband through you at these occasions.'

Whether or not she went to any of the football matches we do not know,
but she was gently invited to consider how her son was also grieving.

There are those who choose to move into family life with that
vulnerable strength that offers who they are, even though they are
hurting. These are the people I find myself truly drawn to, those whose

loneliness is tangible, their struggle is real but it is not tainted by self pity. Only when I have genuinely felt it have I said something like:

> 'I can hear your heartache that comes from the part of your being where you had that relationship with... (name), and nothing else can fill it, but you still continue to be a big part of your family life.'

This has touched into those painful emotions, but at the same time it has been a relief for them to hear their struggle has been recognized. The families of such people will learn from them about loss and pain as well as the reality of struggling to live for others – that can be a great legacy to pass on to any family.

The 'holding onto belongings' strategy: A familiar strategy designed to keep the presence of the loved one near is the keeping of certain possessions and particularly items of clothing. These clothes 'embody the person'; in particular they hold the odour of the loved one, his aftershave, his cologne or deodorant, his sweat, her perfume, hairspray. Perhaps because of some of the thinking we have previously assimilated about bereavement, it might suggest to us that people are making a shrine to the loved one. Perhaps we feel that is a little out of the ordinary, so they need to be encouraged to deal with the belongings and have a clear out. In essence, we think they should 'let go'. At this point we need to remember that people want to hold on to their relationship with the deceased and they do not want to break the bonds.

While we would not talk about letting go, we would talk to them about living with their pain and, at the same time, adjusting to their new life situation. Some people take a longer time than others to make adjustments, and if they want to keep the house as it was for a year or two there is no harm in this. From our experience, we only need to think about grief being more complicated if the person is not able to function because of their grief. Some people live with a sorrow that will always be present; some days will be better than others, and while they are able to live and function, they carry the perpetual sorrow of their loss. So, if people want to hold onto a book collection, clothes, personal belongings or something that was made by the deceased which brings comfort, then we would not try to discourage that strategy if it is working for them. You might simply ask them:

'What comfort do you get from keeping these things?'

It might sound obvious, but remember, do not assume to know what their comfort looks like. In any case, it is really important they articulate it for themselves, to hear their own voice saying what is true for them. A way of following up on this would be to ask:

'When might you envisage a time when you could start to let a few of these things go?'

The 'maintaining contact' strategy: We have talked about the concept that many continue to feel connected to their loved one after the death and some people develop strategies to keep that going. It seems that more and more people are telling me of their visits to spirit mediums. If this is said to me I will try to explore it with something like:

'You've felt the need to try to contact the spirit of your wife. I wonder what it is you're struggling with that you want answered in this way.'

When I have followed it up, I will ask them:

'What measure of comfort has it brought for you, do you think?'

Often they will tell me something specific; the illness or the death was so painful they wanted to know that the deceased is at rest. Sometimes they will tell me the experience was not what they thought it would be and they would not try it again. You can pursue this by exploring what it was they did think it would be. These visits, as with frequent visits to the grave or the place where the ashes are scattered, are ways of trying to keep the person alive in the client's memory. Sometimes there is a need to be 'close', sometimes a need to 'talk' to the loved one. Some people talk to the photograph of their loved one, and may even set up a small memorial place with flowers and candles at home, where they can sit to talk and share. Some people write their daily diaries or journals to their loved one, recalling the day's events and their feelings. These strategies help people to maintain the relationship beyond the grave, and may be perfectly acceptable to them, though perhaps less so to us.

The 'boxing up' strategy: Some people we have met only briefly in our service, because they want to be sure that they have done things 'well'. These people often have 'boxed up' their grief and apparently dealt with it. It is a strategy that will enable that person to 'move on' because that is what they want to do. It might sound as if I am contradicting myself in this instance, but there are people who do want to 'move on'. You can check with them in this way:

> 'I notice you've talked about wanting to move on. How much is that something you feel you want to do for yourself?' You can follow up with:

> 'So what do you think might stop you moving on now?'

It may be that this is their stated goal and their expressed desire for their future. It is difficult to say how successful this strategy is or not, as we do not usually have the opportunity to speak with them for long. It can also be, though not always, part of the desire to find a new partner. They want to make sure the grief for their loved one is dealt with. Perhaps they have believed, or it might be what others have said to them, that if they do not deal with it now, it will come back to haunt them.

The 'keeping angry' strategy: We sometimes meet those whose strategy for coping is to hold onto the anger they have had for the authorities who were involved before the death: it might be the police force, the paramedics, the hospital or the doctor at the local surgery. In Chapter 1 (page 48) we met Elizabeth who had successfully fought her campaign for her son Steve, and while she was campaigning she kept going with the energy her anger provided. Then she won her case, but it could not bring back her son. Blaming the authorities might work for some people as they keep their hearts fired with the anger, but once the anger dissipates they will feel the pain of loss. Feeling anger is preferable to them than feeling the pain of loss which they think they can not cope with. You can ask gently:

> 'How much do you think your anger is keeping you away from feeling your pain?'

We also meet people who are angry with God, though they may have had no previously deeply held religious beliefs. There are those who are angry with themselves which often makes them depressed; and those who feel angry with the deceased for not going to the doctor sooner, not telling them sooner, for leaving them with the mess. There are those who are angry at others, anyone who is around, especially friends who can not do right for doing wrong. Anger works to a point for these people, but it can be quite destructive of other relationships. The woman who criticizes her friends for not calling often enough, or not being there for her, will soon find herself alone completely. You might be able to say after a while of working with someone like this:

> 'You've talked a lot about the anger you feel. I'm just going to try this, and I hope I won't be offending you, but how might your anger be affecting your relationships with others in your family or with your friends?'

I would not attempt to say this without having built up a good rapport with the client, so be sure you do not challenge too soon. I often preface something a little difficult with words that prepare them, 'I hope you won't be offended, but...' They usually take the gentleness of it quite well.

The 'keeping life the same' strategy: Some people will try to get through their grief by living the same life as they had before; they keep to the same routines, and they have the same holidays. They do not want to change their life, even in the light of extreme change. This is different however to those who are in denial about the person's death, those who are carrying on as if the person is not dead. Both these strategies are difficult to handle, for different reasons. The one who carries on the same is not in denial about the death; they want to keep the same routines because it brings them comfort. In other events of life they may have found change difficult, but bereavement is even harder for them to manage. (The families of these people are often more impacted by the lack of change because they see that life can not go on the same.) In this instance, you can point out what you see happening for them:

> 'From what you're telling me, you're trying to keep life exactly the same, with the same routines in your daily life. How is that working for you as a way of coping?'

In fact, they may not have recognized this is a strategy they are using and so by asking something like this, it may help them to understand what they are doing. You may also ask them:

> 'Is this way of coping the right way for you, do you think? Or is there another way you might be able to cope?'

For those in denial of the death, we may need to refer for psychiatric support until they are able to accept the death. We may not meet many of them in any event, because they do not want to acknowledge the death, but their families or doctor might be requesting help.

The 'victim' strategy: Some people we have encountered have a rather distressing way of dealing with their grief, in that they make sure people around them are always aware of their grief and their tears. It feels hard to say this, in a book that is about being sensitive to bereaved people, but we have actually come across those who seem to enjoy the attention their bereavement brings them. They may present to you as the 'victim' in life. That is, their life is worse than anybody else's and they have always had a rough deal. I am not talking about those who have genuinely experienced many sorrows and tragedies in their lives, but I am speaking of those who will want everyone to know about their own pain and will often dismiss the pain of others. The response you have to this person might cause you concern, but it might be the same as some members of the family have. You might find yourself without genuine empathy for this person. Something about the way they behave turns you away from them. They want your sympathy and they seem to be trying to wring it out of you.

This is a difficult strategy to handle as you end up feeling quite alienated by the person, and it may need some very gentle work to get them to see that what they are doing is having the opposite effect to what they want. However, as I know from many years of practice, these people have probably been like this for a long time, even before their bereavement, and nothing much will change it. Indeed, if you try to openly challenge their way of being, you will probably end up being accused of being against them, and they will stop seeing you. This is a situation when you may feel the need to talk about this person in your supervision, to handle the negative thoughts you are having about this client. At least expressing your feelings and exploring them without being judged will be of benefit to you.

The 'self-destructive' strategy: Unfortunately there are those whose strategies and ways of coping are self destructive; sometimes we meet those who turn to excessive drinking, smoking, eating with or without bulimic tendencies, or anorexic problems. We find these hard to handle, and sometimes people have been in these patterns before the death occurred. If I know about the drinking habit of the one who has asked for support I will explain to them that I can not allow a bereavement support worker to visit while they might be under the influence of alcohol. I have known clients who wanted to have support agree not to drink before their support worker arrives. They made their appointments early enough so that if they wanted a drink at lunch time they could. We are not going to alter the habit of an already heavy drinker but the sessions can help them come to terms with their loss in an appropriate way. If a support worker arrives to find their client has been drinking, then I have told them to explain they can not stay under these circumstances, and to leave as quietly as they can. They are then to make contact with me before arranging another visit, so that I can make the call to the client to explain. It is too serious to have lone workers at risk in vulnerable places with people who might be out of control or who may act irrationally. Sometimes we need to bring in other agencies to help, if the client is willing to receive the help. If you have set it up in your initial working agreement or contract with the client, you can go back to it by saying something like:

> 'When I first started seeing you, I mentioned that if I felt you needed further expert support then I would talk to you about getting that support. I believe the issue around your (e.g. drinking/eating/self harming) … is deeper rooted than I am qualified to handle and I would suggest you think about allowing us to make a referral back to your doctor, who can talk to you about further support for this particular issue.'

Whatever the destructive strategy, you will need to talk it through with your supervisor and ensure that you have the correct support or the ability to refer on to another agency.

The 'self-help' strategy: There are many people who have been bereaved who are aware that they have got to help themselves. They will read books, they will sign up to new courses, they will start going to churches where there are midweek group meetings, they will join self-help groups, support groups or social groups that are designed especially for a bereaved person. These people are eager to share and want to be with others who have experienced similar situations and where they do not have to explain too many things because they can feel understood. This can feel very positive and we do need to affirm these people in their efforts, not forgetting, however, that when they close the door after these events they are still left with their loss. You can explore this with them by asking them:

'What kind of help are the support groups being for you?' Or,

'When you get back from your support activities, how do you handle things then?'

It would be a mistake to suggest to them that they are doing really well and should, for instance, be thinking of volunteering in a local charitable concern or returning to work. We can hurry people up too much, and with this type of person we can assume they are in a different emotional place to where they really are.

The 'humour' strategy: Perhaps we have come across in our lives those who play the part of the perpetual joker; it is the role they have played out in the family, or at school and work for most of their lives. The place of humour of course is mixed. It can be used to ease tension, or think about things in a different way. If humour is the only way someone deals with death, though, then it can be a source of irritation to other family members and a hindrance to the one who is grieving. They are not allowing themselves the space to be sad in the presence of others. Some gentle challenging of this might be helpful:

'I've noticed that you seem to make a joke when we start talking seriously about your wife, which gets us away from the subject. I wonder if you're aware of doing that.'

The above description of some of the strategies we have encountered is not exhaustive, but these seem to be some of the most common ones. When we listen to the bereaved person we start to identify what it is they are doing to cope with their grief. We are also aware that there are swings of 'moods' that people go into. They can be coping quite well and then something happens, or does not happen, and they are in the depths of distress.

In giving us a clearer understanding of this phenomenon, the work of Stroebe and Schut (1999) has proved to be beneficial. They presented a model which they call the 'Dual Process Model' that describes two orientations: one that describes the stress around loss, and the other that describes what people do when they are trying to rebuild their lives. These two orientations are on the one hand 'loss' and on the other 'restoration'. It is evident that coping does not occupy all of a bereaved person's time: 'coping is embedded in everyday life experience, which involves taking time off from grieving, as when watching an engrossing TV program, reading, talking with friends about some other topic, or sleeping' (p.212). Stroebe and Schut describe the 'loss orientation' as the time when the bereaved person is mainly dealing with or processing some aspect of the loss experience. During this time they will be focusing on the relationship, the tie, or bond with the deceased, they might experience deep yearning for the deceased and become distressed. It is also pointed out: 'Early on in bereavement, loss orientation dominates, later on, attention turns more and more to other sources of upheaval and distress' (p.213).

In the 'restoration orientation' the bereaved person is responding to their new life situation, and they might be focusing on what needs to be dealt with, in a practical manner. They may be making some adjustments to the way of life that is now required of them, and attempting to manage some of the tasks the deceased used to do, such as the finances, the shopping, the cooking, coping with plumbing and electrical problems. They may be avoiding the emotional side of their grief in order to begin to bring about the reorganization of their life they know must happen. They might be undertaking the development of a new identity from being a married person to being a widowed person, or from being a parent of a living child to being the parent of a deceased child. Stroebe and Schut describe a 'dynamic process', that is, it changes and moves as the bereaved person alternates between the loss and restoration orientations. It is not a question of 'either/or', but rather a 'back-and-forth' process between the two, confronting and avoiding at various times, given certain circumstances and new triggers.

I find the two models, the one describing grief patterns (Martin and Doka) and the other describing the oscillation in the dual process (Stroebe and Schut), describe well how people are managing their grief. You will see in the section on techniques that I have taken the Dual Process Model and have developed the exercise on bad and good days. The client can begin to understand how they fit into some kind of identified pattern which demonstrates the rollercoaster experience they tell us they go through. The explanation of the oscillation between the two orientations assists us in understanding our experience that people can be different from session to session. In fact, we would perhaps be more concerned if we did not hear that people had their ups and downs and experiences of waves of sorrow, followed by times of productive sorting out and getting on with life. It is perhaps a way of coping that enables the person to keep mentally well, rather than being entirely in one orientation all the time.

WHAT DO YOU DO WITH THE STRATEGY FOR COPING?

Key Listening Activity: Understand and affirm it or challenge it.

It is often through the stories about how the client is now, that you can deduce many things about how they are coping. They may start by telling you how they are *not* coping. Of course, in a sense that is why they have usually requested support. Some may think that they are not coping when in fact they are experiencing the normal reactions of a grieving person: lethargy, lack of interest, no energy, lack of concentration, short span of attention, physical nausea or sickness, tightness in the chest and anxiety.

Even when you explore with those who say they are not coping, you can usually identify some strategies, but they are usually ones that are not working well. As we have seen above, there are many ways of coping. So, it is important to try to understand the way they are coping so that we can explore with them whether it is a strategy that is working for them. If the strategies they are using are not working for them, then you need to be able to challenge them in a gentle way to see how things can be done differently.

I am going to risk repeating something here, because I consider that it is worth repeating at this point in particular. When thinking about coping strategies, it would be easy to fall into the 'fixing' mode, trying to sort out our clients' lives for them. We need to be careful to avoid falling into the trap of making all sorts of suggestions for them, and advising them in all sorts of creative ways. If you find yourself doing this, you will soon hear the client putting up resistance to your suggestions, like, 'I can't get there because I don't drive.' Or, 'That's on a Tuesday and I look

after my granddaughter that day, so I wouldn't be able to do that.'
Trying to sort our clients out is not a strategy that works for us as support
workers.

What we have learnt by taking note of the theory about different
grief patterns is that we have to be cautious when we are thinking about
how people cope with their grief. First, we need to be careful not to
think that everyone should cry in their grief. Just because people do not
shed tears does not mean there is no grief or pain. There are people who
will ask for support because they have not cried and they wonder what is
wrong with them, and they feel their family is thinking they do not care
for the loved one. Sometimes we need to work out with them how they
have managed in other circumstances, and whether they have been able
to cry at other times in their lives. Often by getting them to tell their
stories, to talk about the relationship they had, to celebrate the life and
focus on the legacy left behind they will find themselves experiencing
tears and sadness. Some people need the time and space to talk about
their loved one in order to begin to feel. Sometimes, we find that not
crying has actually been a person's way of coping with something as
traumatic as this. If we identify this pattern for them they can sometimes
feel the freedom not to cry, which can be a relief in itself. So, the quantity
of tears shed does not indicate the level of pain felt.

Second, we also have to be cautious about discounting the strategies
people have for their survival. We may have our own thoughts about
how people should be going about their grieving, and if they are not
doing it in this way, we might find we are dismissing something that is
really important for them. That is why we do not go into these
discussions with preconceived notions of what grief looks like. Finding
out what is going on for the person in front of us is important. It is better
to ask ourselves, and them, some questions:

> How do they want to do it?
>
> What have they been experiencing?
>
> Where do they need help to rethink some of their strategies?

It might be that someone is putting off coming to terms with the reality
of the death because they have got other concerns to cope with that are
going to take up their energy. I remember the client whose wife died

after their third child was born, and he had to concentrate on supporting that new life as well as looking after his other two children and their grief. So he did not have enough emotional resources to consider the full impact of his wife's death until a long time after the child's birth. We would have made a grave error in dismissing his way of handling his bereavement if we had wanted to 'work' on his grief before he was ready and able to do so.

Third, we have to be cautious about wanting the client to do something in another way. Because we are all different it means that we are going to respond differently. If I had talked to Frank about pounding his pain out on the treadmill as an addictive type of behaviour, something not to be done in excess, I would have missed out on what he was saying. For him, even though it was excessive, and even though it took him away from his family at that time, his pain was so overwhelming he wanted to get the hurt out. It worked for him. It might not have been what I would have wanted him to do, as I had some concerns for his adult children. He did not want to talk at great length about his feelings; he felt the need to 'do' something. He could not help his adult children either because he had to deal with his pain on his own. I had to respect that, even though I was aware there may be a sadness experienced by the children in that family as they could not talk about their pain to him.

So our listening activity at this point is to understand the strategy and either affirm it, if it is working well, or challenge it, if it is not. We can probably deduce how people are operating as we listen carefully to how they are telling us their stories. In fact, you probably will not have much trouble identifying the client who operates in the intuitive pattern, as they identify themselves. They are the ones who are telling you how it feels and how it is for them. These people will respond well to talking about their pain and their loss as they have someone to share with when you are there. Perhaps their family members are not so eager to listen because of their own patterns of coping. The challenge for this person would be in thinking about how others in the family might be coping and how to help them. You might also, eventually, challenge them gently into thinking about how they can turn their attention towards making some cognitive plans for adjusting to the situation. You could do it this way:

'During our sessions, you've talked a great deal about how you feel and how it is for you in your grief. I wonder if in this session, we might begin to look at how you can start making some small plans for the immediate future and what that might mean for you.'

It is not all that difficult either to identify the instrumental pattern. As soon as you ask how they 'feel', you will get back a thought, an action or something that does not relate at all to what you have asked. It is not as if they are immune to feelings, and do not know what they are; they just do not usually express those feelings in words. Do not expect them to be able to tell you how they are feeling. We need to be careful of discounting this person's way of coping, as if it were less valid than the intuitive pattern. We can usually identify this strategy because they will tell us about how they are doing things, what they've been thinking about, and how they have tackled certain jobs. For people who operate in this cognitive way we can ask:

'How did that impact you?'

'What were you thinking about when that happened?'

'What are you planning to do in the next week?'

'How are you managing with… (e.g. the loneliness, the long nights, going out on your own, meeting with friends on your own)?'

If we speak to this person at this level we will probably obtain all the information we need to support them. It may be difficult, however, for some of us who want to explore the emotions. They may be receptive to some of the more practical things to do with their grief. They may be open to writing an 'unsent letter' though it will have to be relevant for them, and they may be open to creating a life-story book, or writing out their own life stories. I spoke to a woman about how she was getting on, and in great detail she was able to tell me what she had been doing since her husband's death. Then she talked about the fact that she was writing a book. I enquired what it was about. She told me it was her life story, as she'd become aware that her own children and grandchildren didn't seem to know very much about the Second World War. She'd served with the Women's Land Army and she'd had many an adventure that she could tell, so she was treating it as her project by typing it up for them, chapter by chapter. In this way they would have her and her husband's stories. Through this she was getting her own form of therapy and I was not at all surprised that she had decided she did not need any further support.

WHAT QUESTIONS CAN YOU ASK?

We can positively explore the kind of strategies that people are using by asking:

> What are some of the ways you think you're using to help you cope?
>
> How have you responded in the past to losses (or life's difficulties – if there haven't been any other losses)?
>
> What are you doing differently now to what you were doing just after... (name)'s death?
>
> What sort of things have you found useful in helping you through difficult times in the past?
>
> What have you understood about the way you go from one mood to another? How is that different to the way you would normally cope with life?
>
> If you could give a name to the way you're coping, what would it be?

In response to those behaviour patterns that might not be helpful, you can ask:

> How has that been for you?
>
> How helpful have you found that way of coping to be?
>
> What kind of benefit have you found that to be?
>
> How effective have you found that as a way of coping?

When we talk about challenging behaviours, we are not talking about being so confrontational with people that they take offence; we are simply going to ask some questions that perhaps friends and family might not ask. This is not difficult to do; some simple examples might be:

> What other ways might there be of coping with that problem?
>
> What might you be able to do differently?

How would you like to be managing your time (your day, your hours, your week, your weekends, your down times)?

What might you do when you feel you're going to be overwhelmed by your emotions?

What sort of things might you be able to do that would stop you from over-eating/having too much to drink/smoking too much?

In response to some of the answers they might give you:

What might stop you from doing those more positive things?

For those you identify as using an 'instrumental' pattern of coping, instead of asking how something makes them 'feel', ask:

How did you respond or react?

What was going on for you when that happened?

What were your thoughts about that?

How did you manage that?

This enables the person to talk about feelings or thoughts or actions, as they wish.

WHAT TECHNIQUES CAN YOU USE?

The Blob Tree: Make sure you both have one of the diagrams in front of you (see Figure 5.1). Ask the client to pick out one of the 'Blob' figures they think represents themselves and where they are now in their grief. Then ask them to describe what it is about that figure they identify with. You then make observations about the place of the figure in relationship to the tree and where it is in relationship to others. As in the work with stones, try not to interpret for your client; simply make observations and let them discover the connections for themselves. You can also ask them to pick out figures for the other members of the family and think about where they are in relation to the tree and themselves, and then explore how it might be for them to be there. This is sometimes quite impacting for the client in that they can see the whole family in relation to them-selves and what they might be doing.

Figure 5.1 The Blob Tree

Copyright Pip Wilson and Ian Long from 'Games without Frontiers' isbn: 0-551-01554-3 published by Marshall Pickering, imprint of Harper Collins Publishing. Not to be published without written permission from: pip@pipwilson.com www.blobtree.com

'Bad Day, Good Day' exercise: Give your client a piece of paper and a pen, and ask them to divide it into two columns. At the top of the left hand column, write 'When I have a bad day, I...'; and at the top of the right hand column, write 'When I have a good day, I...' Ask them to list as many of the things they experience under each of the headings. You can use these lists to help them think about the ways they manage their bereavement. You can ask questions like:

'What sort of pattern is there to these "days"?'

'How long in between the "days" do you find there is?'

'What sort of things can send you into a "bad day"?'

'How do you get out of a "bad day"?'

An example of a 'Bad Day, Good Day' exercise is given in Figure 5.2.

"When I have a bad day I..."	**When I have a good day I..."**
get up with a head ache	*can think about other things*
start to cry and can't stop	*do the housework*
think of him all day	*do the garden*
feel overwhelmed by the pain	*sort things out*
feel tired	*try to think positively*
miss him	*go shopping*
long to touch him	*meet friends*
don't want to go on	*can think about him without crying*
can't believe it's happened	*can think about what he would want me to do*
	think about what plans to make for the future

Figure 5.2 An example of a 'Bad Day, Good Day' exercise

Buttons and stones: If you have not already used buttons or stones (as described in Chapter 2) when exploring the relationships in the family, you could use them here to look at how people are coping with their grief within the family. Ask the client to select a button or stone that describes how they are in their grief, and then to select other stones for the other family members and ask them to place them in such a way as to show how they are relating to each other. This can lead you and them to explore what is going on for each person, including themselves, as they are grieving in the family.

IMPACT ON YOU AS A LISTENER

As I have mentioned above, one thing that might be going on for you as you talk about how people are coping is that you could be drawn into trying to solve the problem for them, with comments like, 'Have you thought about…' or 'I would suggest you…' If you find yourself doing that, then ask:

> 'What is it about this person or their situation that has made me move into this way of responding?'

Maybe you are looking for a short cut because someone else you saw did this thing and they were greatly helped, so you thought you would offer it as a suggestion. Maybe you feel that your suggestion is exactly what you think they need to do, and of course, they rarely agree with you. This is good material to take to supervision, because something is going on between you and the client that means you have been pulled into solving their problem. Maybe they are playing the part of the 'victim' and drawing you in to be their 'rescuer', their wonderful helper who has the answer! Maybe it is something about this person that reminds you of someone else you saw, or someone else in your life and you were in the role of 'fixer' then. It feels good, let's face it, to be able to fix things for people and sort out their problems. It is not helpful, however, in the long term as people have to come to their own conclusions. It is far more powerful for them to come to their own conclusions about what to do, and then they usually act on them. If you have identified that this is generally your way of responding to people's situations, then perhaps you need to talk it over with your supervisor and try to find what lies behind this 'pull' to work things out for people as it is not helpful to those who need real support.

Another impact of supporting people in their grief is that you might not be able to fully appreciate how they are surviving and making necessary adjustments. As you work with bereavement you can become a little desensitized to the amount of effort and courage it takes to live with the pain of death. Death is truly an enemy of the human condition and we do not fight it on a level battlefield. In identifying how people cope and their ways of relearning their worlds, an antidote to desensitization could be to allow yourself to marvel at how they cope from day to day. 'Living from day to day' is not just an adage; it is a reality for them. We can appreciate their fortitude and their determination, and we can encourage them in their times of battle weariness.

One of the things I find personally distressing is the awful loneliness people often talk about. It is the kind of loneliness that does not pass with social gatherings of friends or family, so no amount of company will fill the gap. Whatever they try to do, whatever strategies they use, they may continue to feel some measure of that soul loneliness. I find myself saddened because it is a real emptiness, a dark void that is left behind, and I think about how I would cope. I know that as I listen to their heartache, it comes from the place where there is sometimes desolation. When we are impacted by their pain, it is good to be able to acknowledge it to ourselves and to others in supervision, and even to the client if appropriate.

In summary:

- Martin and Doka (1999) suggest that there are several healthy ways of coping with grief rather than stereotyping men and women into gender specific responses. They describe three specific patterns: an 'intuitive pattern', an 'instrumental pattern', and a 'blended pattern'.

- People should be assisted to identify how they cope and to think about how each pattern has its strengths and its weaknesses.

- Stroebe and Schut (1999) presented the Dual Process Model which illustrates the phenomenon of being on a rollercoaster. They describe two orientations, one that shows how the person is when focusing on their loss, and the other that demonstrates what people do when they are trying to rebuild their lives.

- People go between the two orientations, confronting their loss and avoiding it at various times, given certain circumstances and new triggers.

- There are practical strategies that people use either consciously or unconsciously, some of which are: protective, keeping busy, getting fit, fund raising, taking care of others, isolation and withdrawal, holding onto belongings, maintaining contact, boxing up, keeping angry, keeping life the same, being the victim, being self destructive, self help, and humour.

- The listening activity is to understand what strategy the person is using to cope and either affirm it or challenge it if it is not working for the client.

CHAPTER 6

Element 6: There is a journey undertaken

- ❀ There is a story
- ❀ There is a relationship
- ❀ There is a life to celebrate
- ❀ There is a legacy left behind
- ❀ There is a strategy for coping
- ❀ **There is a journey undertaken**

In the past I have loved travelling, moving from England to Italy, to South Africa, America and back. At that time, I loved the actual journeys, the coaches, the trains, the planes and I am blessed in not being travel sick. I would study the scenery, think of the people's lives behind the walls of their houses (or shacks) and be intrigued by the different architecture in the various different cultures. As people we all need the same things in life to live and yet we all do it differently, depending on the terrain, where we have been placed geographically in the world. However, as I have got older the journeys no longer seem to be as enthralling for me; I am more interested now in the destination – in getting there. What has happened, I wonder, to the interest I had as a younger woman? Maybe it is about age, and the journeys which are more uncomfortable for my body. Perhaps I am more accustomed to the scenery and take it for granted. Perhaps where I am going is more important because of the people I am going to see again or meet for the first time?

As I think about this I am aware that this might be how some of our bereaved people feel. People live out their grief differently; sometimes depending on the geographical and cultural constraints and norms, sometimes depending on their own life situations, the 'terrain' of life that surrounds them at the time. If they are older, they may now be longing for another place, to be with their loved ones, life's journey has lost its appeal, they are tired; they want to get to where they are going. If they are younger they might be more inclined to wonder what is going on in their lives. Life ahead feels more uncertain than it did. They have perhaps lost their way, lost direction. The one who was directing them, offering stability and guidance along the way, is no longer there. They could find themselves in foreign territory and it is scary. They do not know how to live in this place of grief and sorrow; it is like nothing they have ever encountered before.

You might pause here to think about the client's journey. Here are some pointers to help you:

1. Reflect on what you would expect to see at the start of the journey of grief.

2. What would you expect to hear from people as the experience of their loss becomes more of a reality to them?

3. Consider what you would expect to hear from people as they are further along in their journey towards some measure of adjustment to their changed life circumstance.

When trying to plot this journey of grief, it has been helpful for me to look at the work of two psychologists, Colin Murray Parkes and William Worden, who have something to say about the themes that are part of the landscape for bereaved people. As both provide four steps, I will look at each one separately, making comments and observations along the way about what we (the bereavement team) have experienced in our own practice. It has been interesting to see how there has been some overlay of our experiences and their observations of the phases and tasks.

Parkes (1998) talks about four phases of grieving through which people will travel. The first phase is the distress experienced at the time of the death which is usually followed by numbness lasting for hours or days. Because we are not normally present at that early stage immediately after a death, we do not come across this numbness very often. Our experience is that many are grappling with the reality of the death and are still trying to process it as something real.

Worden's work is based around four 'tasks of mourning' (1991) which are formulated on the understanding that there are positive things to be done in order that the bereaved person regains some balance in their life. His assumption is that throughout our lives our human growth and development are influenced by various tasks. He maintains that each of these tasks needs to be completed so that growth can take place. The first task he identifies is that people need 'to accept the reality of the loss' (p.10). This seems a little obvious but there are some people who struggle with this. When we see people soon after a death, they are often wrestling with the stark reality of the event, and acceptance does seem to be the first step along the journey for them. They struggle with the dream-like quality or nightmare they feel they are in, and that when they wake up they will still have their loved one. We hear, 'I still can't believe he's gone.' It does not feel real to them. This does not mean they are in denial though; it is part of trying to come to terms with the enormity of the loss.

Parkes speaks of the second phase as a time of intense feelings, when they can experience a deep yearning and longing for the deceased. There can also be periodic pangs of grief, brought on by the acute sense of separation which they might experience between their normal daily activities and daily routines. He believes that they might still be able to continue with the essential tasks of life though these may be done without much energy and with anxiety. Sometimes there are physical symptoms that can accompany this phase: 'All appetites are diminished, weight is lost, concentration and short term memory are diminished, and as time goes by the bereaved person often becomes irritable and depressed' (p.19). What we see at the start of the journey with bereaved people seems to match up quite well with what Parkes speaks of here. We might expect to hear confused thinking, thoughts that are not totally rational or consistent. In this emotional place along the journey there can be various feelings expressed. Sometimes we hear relief – relief that the waiting is over, the trauma of the illness is over. This is a transient feeling before they move into the deeper experience of loss. Or we might hear guilt, 'Could I have done more?' This might be followed by the frequently heard, 'I should have...' – 'I should have been there at the end.'

Worden's second task of mourning is 'to work through to the pain of grief' (p.13). He believes that the pain of loss should be felt and not avoided otherwise it might be that they will need help at a later time. In practice, we experience the client's struggle to come through this place of pain. They move in and out of the pain, and yet it is always present in some way. We often hear the self blaming, and blaming of others in the family, as they analyse in minute detail the days or weeks before and after the death. Certainly we may hear, 'If only...' – 'If only I'd been able to get him to go to the doctor sooner, he might still be alive today.' These might come as a torrent of thoughts and recriminations, of self scrutiny, trying to make sense of it. If you are working with a sudden death or suicide survivor your work here can be quite long term; these doubts and recriminations are not dealt with in one or two sessions. Another theme at the start of this journey seems to be a questioning whether they are normal in their responses because they feel as if they are going mad. They want to check out if what they are feeling is in line with what others also feel.

Parkes' third phase describes disorganization and despair setting in. This phase may be a time of looking for ways of trying to put things right by going over and over the events. 'The memory of the dead person is never far away' (p.20) and it may be that the bereaved person sees or hears the deceased, though these 'hallucinations' disappear as soon as the bereaved person wakes up from sleep or daydreaming. In our experience, also, as their journey progresses the reality of their loss sinks in. It seems harder for people months after the death than it was at the beginning. So we can expect people to be talking as if life is not worth living and that they experience very dark times. It might worry us that people seem to be going downhill, but this is part of the journey for them and they are describing the downside of the rollercoaster ride. Some report the onset of dreams of the deceased, and perhaps, as Parkes indicates, the presence of the deceased comes to them in a dream or when they are half asleep. Feeling the presence can bring comfort to them or it may signify that they want to deal with unfinished business. This is a point you might need to bring up:

> 'I sense you might be a little confused about this experience. I wonder if there is something that's not quite finished for you that needs to be addressed here.'

Talking to the deceased can also be a frequently reported aspect of this part of the journey.

Worden's third task of mourning is 'to adjust to an environment in which the deceased is missing' (p.14). He talks of the adjustment that has to be made in the life of the bereaved person, as well as having to face the challenges of coming to terms with their new status and identity. In practice, we also hear about the painful adjustments and challenges that they are facing at this place in the journey. Some people describe it as being 'in their own world', where they feel they are the only ones who are grieving. They look around and see others in life getting on, laughing, shopping, going out, dancing, working. In all of this they feel isolated, in a bubble, lonely in a crowd. They make comparisons with others, some being shocked by the intensity of envy they feel towards others who have still got their partners, their children, their parents.

Parkes states 'the phases of grieving should not be regarded as a rigid sequence that is passed through only once' (p.20). He considers that passing backwards and forwards between pining and despair (phases two and three) can be gone through many times. This is something that we can concur with, and because of it we do not make hasty assessments based on a single session when the client may be feeling in a good place. Rather than finishing the work with them, we would try increasing the weeks between sessions and see how they are after a few more weeks have elapsed, so they have more of a gauge of how they are coping.

Parkes speaks of the final phase as a time of reorganization and return to some level of normal functioning, with the pangs of grief becoming less frequent. In our experience we might begin to hear people asking the question, 'Where do I go from here?' You might also hear them say things like, 'I know I've got to make some changes.' This could be a sign that there is a measure of beginning to make an adjustment. Perhaps they think about changing things in the house, or garden. They might have thought long and hard about moving house, which can be a loss of the memories for some, but a need to be out of the place of memories for others.

Worden's fourth task is 'to emotionally relocate the deceased and move on with life' (p.16). He believes it is necessary to be able to create an emotional place for the deceased in the heart and mind of the bereaved so that they might be able to function and live in their new world. In our experience this part of the journey is not a question of moving on, as I have discussed before. What we do experience, however, is that people seem to begin to carry their loved one's memory in another place; it is no longer at the forefront of their thinking day in day out. They might start to deal with their loved one's possessions, though this in itself does not necessarily indicate that someone is coming to terms with their loss. For some it is indeed an indicator of making adjustments and making space, both literally and metaphorically, a decision to find their own place. (For others it might be so as not to find their loved one's clothes and possessions around, which might take them into emotions they fear they can not control. These people have not come to Worden's fourth task yet.) A good indicator of beginning to live in their new world is when they can talk about those memorable moments without being paralysed by their grief. Tears are not necessarily an indicator that someone can not control their grief. There may be tears for a long time to come. When they do not hinder the person's general ability to function reasonably well then the client might be making some adjustments. You might find someone on this part of their journey talking about the tough times and tender moments, reflecting realistically about their life and their loved one.

I value what Worden says about the ambivalence of the journey after bereavement when he summed it up in this way: 'There is a sense in which mourning can be finished, when people regain an interest in life, feel more hopeful, experience gratification again, and adapt to new roles. There is also a sense in which mourning is never finished' (p.19). In our experience the route a journey takes is not a straight line. We see that people more often go round in circles rather than a straight line. Most people eventually come to a place of more settled adjustment and a place where they might learn to live and grow without the physical presence of their loved one.

As we look at the way we communicate with people in their grief we will use the analogy of the journey to help them gain a different perspective on what is going on for them. Perhaps they will be encouraged to see a bigger picture of their journey and life. Let's take a look now at some of the ways our bereaved clients have described their journeys and what we might do with those metaphors.

The rollercoaster: Many describe their journey as a rollercoaster with ups and downs; good days and bad days. The rollercoaster is the image of the thrilling ride at the fun fair, but in this context the client will say it is more like a nightmare. They do not like it; they are tired and often exhausted by it. If they talk about being on a rollercoaster early on in your sessions, you might ask them:

> 'What's the worst part of this rollercoaster ride for you?'

Then you might follow up with:

> 'How do you know when you're travelling on the upside of the ride?'

If you are near the end of your sessions with them and you know you are going to be coming to a close, you might ask them:

> 'What have you learnt from this rollercoaster experience?'

We have often heard they have realized that when they are down they know it won't last that long; it won't take as long as it used to before they start going up again. They have told us that when they first set out on the journey, they were terrified of these down days; they would seem to go on for long dark periods. But gradually they were more able to predict that tomorrow or the day after tomorrow they would begin to come up again. You can also use the imagery around the metaphor, and ask things like:

> 'When you were up at the top of the ride, what could you see from there?'

This will really stretch them into making the metaphor work for them. Maybe they will say they've seen that the way ahead isn't so bleak, that there is a little relief from the darkness; they've seen some of the light ahead. You can then talk about what they have seen as light; what might have helped them see some light. It might just be that they have had an enjoyable day out with some friends and they laughed together over something, and spent it in good heart. We are not looking for big leaps in discovery here, only small things to count as achievements.

The river. Some have talked about being in a river. They describe being pushed or pulled along by its strong current. They have experienced being dragged down by reeds and things in the way, and they have talked about feeling as if they are drowning. These images are evocative and can be used creatively as you think through what it means to be in the river. You could ask:

> 'Who or what is doing the pushing or pulling?'

> 'What does the current feel like?'

> 'How are you managing to stay afloat?'

> 'What happens when you feel you're drowning?'

> 'When are the times when you feel like drowning?'

> 'What are the reeds that try to bring you down?'

> 'Who might help you get out of the river?'

> 'What would you need to do to get out?'

Some of these questions might prove helpful to bring them into a creative problem-solving mode.

The 'long and winding' road: Some have talked about the road that seems to wind on and on, with no end in sight, and being enveloped in darkness. Again here are some useful ways of developing the metaphor in order for people to apply it to their real experience:

> 'What does the darkness feel like?'

> 'Is it completely black or can you see shadows and shades of grey around?'

> 'How many people are on this road with you?'

Of course, they might just see themselves on the road alone, but you might be able to bring other members of the family in who are also experiencing the loss.

> 'What might there be at the side of the road to help you? – I'm thinking of a lay-by where you might pull in and rest. – What might that be for you?'

> 'Are there any crossroads or turn-offs on this road?'

> 'What sign posts might you look for?'

The railway track: Some have talked about the railway track they are on, which they can't get off because it is leading them in a direction that is already fixed. They might talk about going through dark tunnels, or seeing the light at the end of the tunnel. This is similar in a way to the road and river where they feel they are powerless to stop something happening in their lives. The feeling of powerlessness can be overwhelming; they are not in control of what is happening to them, and some force greater than them is at work. You might creatively ask things like:

> 'Are there any stations along the way for you to stop at?'

> 'What prevents you getting off the train at any of these stations?'

> 'What scenery might you see on the train?'

> 'What have the tunnels meant to you?'

> 'What is the light at the end of the tunnel?'

A tidal ebb and flow: Some talk about their journey in terms of the ebb and flow of the tide and speak of their pain coming over them like waves, which again conjures up the picture that they do not feel in control and don't know when the pain of grief is coming. I would suggest that here you can ask:

> 'When the tide is ebbing away, what does it feel like?'

> 'How long does it seem to be between the tides?'

> 'What sort of signs might you see as the tide is coming towards you?'

> 'What is the wave about for you?'

'What happens when the wave hits you?'

The whirlpool (similar ones are the 'quicksand', the 'earthquake or tsunami', the 'maze'): Though strictly speaking these metaphors do not represent the journey as much as they depict the emotional state of the client, they are worth mentioning here, and certainly can be useful in exploring with the client. The first of these metaphors conjures up the picture of a massive event that has happened in the life of the client: the whirlpool – a surge of water that is pulling the client in and down. Some exploration of this could be:

'What sort of things are like the water pulling you down?'

'Where might the water pull you down to?'

'What would you be most afraid of in this whirlpool?'

The second, the quicksand:

'What is this quicksand made up of?'

'What is its power to suck you in?'

'What might you look for in the middle of the quicksand to help you?'

The third, the earthquake or tsunami:

'What does the landscape look like in your earthquake (your tsunami)?'

'Where are you in the picture of your earthquake (your tsunami)?'

'How is it for you there?'

'What do you need to get out of there?'

The above examples are some of the metaphors we have come across with our clients when talking about their journeys. It is worth noting that at this point for them, we are alongside them in their journey. As we listen to, and are indeed even a part of, their journey, we might be able to detect certain themes that show up as 'sign posts' along the way. What I mean is that there may be things that help you see where they might be. One of our bereavement team says she thinks she knows when it is time to move towards finishing with a client when they start to talk about other people's concerns and even begin asking questions about her. She says it is as if they turn from themselves and begin to look outward to others. It has proved to be a good sign post for her.

WHAT DO YOU DO WITH THE JOURNEY UNDERTAKEN?

> Key Listening Activity: Chart their pathway
> and accompany them on their journey.

What do I mean by 'charting their pathway'? As bereaved people will often describe themselves as being in 'a fog', it is perhaps part of our support of them to keep a check on where they are going, and where they have been. To that end, I think we need to be quite careful about what we are given and keep in mind what we have heard. You would need to keep notes that tell you what you have discussed in each session, and your organization can guide you in this, but part of the note-taking can be charting their pathway. Along the way ask yourself these questions:

> Where is their journey taking them?

> What part of the journey are you listening to?

Are there repetitive themes and subjects that keep coming up that need to be dealt with?

Perhaps you have not noticed or acknowledged something for them and they are bringing it up (yet again). If this is the case, put it to them:

> 'I notice that you've mentioned... (e.g. your brother-in-law's part in the funeral) before. I wonder if there's something you want to explore about that or if there's something troubling you about it.'

It is good to think actively about their journey. This is where frequent reviewing of the six elements can be quite helpful. You can do this in your notes, on your own, before you go into the session with the client; or you can do your review in a supervision session. Ask yourself some questions as you look over the sessions with your client:

What have you learnt?

What is still unclear for you?

Do you have a clear picture of the deceased?

Do you understand their story?

What do you recall about the death?

What kind of relationship did they have?

What sort of things does your client value about the deceased, and what are the legacies they left behind?

Are you aware of how the client is coping and what they're struggling with?

If these things are clear in your mind, your own journey with the client is on good firm footing, and my thoughts are that you will have been doing some good work, and the client will feel safe to explore even more, if there is more. If you are not clear, then there is perhaps more work to do in getting the picture clearer, and you might need to be honest and say:

'I'm not sure I've got such a good picture of... Would you be able to go back to that and talk about it some more?'

Remember, if you are not clear in your own mind (and it is not just a problem with your memory) then perhaps the client is still a little foggy about things too.

The use of the six elements, and particularly the journey, can be helpful when you need to ask about continuing or finishing. If you feel you have got good and full answers to the above questions and you do not know where you go now, it might be worth raising it with your client. First, do a brief summary of what you have discussed (in terms of the elements), and then, second, question as to what they feel they would want to talk about in future sessions. Here is an example:

'We've covered a lot of ground and I feel as if I've really got to know Fred and your life together. You've talked about what he meant to you and the family; the good things about him and some of his ways. You've talked about how his humour seems to have been passed on in the family and how his love of Christmas especially will live on in the way your family do things. We've talked about your struggles, the loneliness and the pain of living without him. I wonder now what more you would like to talk about, if we were to make a few more sessions?'

So, you are charting their pathway and you have accompanied them on their way. As I have talked about the different metaphors for the journey, I have also given examples of various questions you might ask, which allow them to think through the journey they are on. In this way you accompany them: you have not left them on their journey without walking alongside them for a while.

Let's look at some practical things about using this element of the journey, which you might want to consider. There is the issue of timing. I would suggest that you do not start your conversation by talking about the 'grief journey' because you really need to know about the deceased, the stories and the relationship. It also may feel too daunting for people as they consider this might be a long journey, especially those of a melancholic disposition. If I am asked, 'How long will it take? Will I always feel like this?' then naturally I will try to be honest by saying something like:

> 'Everyone's different in the way they handle their grief and I don't think I can possibly say how long it'll be for you. You've experienced a major event in your life, and life is going to be different from now on.'

I would not necessarily talk about the journey with people who have been recently bereaved (a few weeks or a couple of months); they have not travelled enough of the journey to usefully reflect on it. However, one useful way of using this element is to introduce the metaphor about their journey at the time you do a review. (We do reviews with our clients generally speaking at about the fourth or sixth sessions. This enables us to recap on where they are; find out what is going on in the sessions, whether they are proving to be helpful, what in particular might have been most helpful; and whether the client would like to continue with the sessions or not.) If you bring the metaphor in at this point it may help them, and you, to get an idea of where they think they are. Then you can introduce the same metaphor in your concluding session, identifying what changes the client might see in their journey now, in contrast with what they talked about before.

There is also the issue of finding yourself 'stuck' with a client and you do not feel you are making much headway in the sense of moving through the elements. When we look at this in supervision, very often the support worker's feeling reflects the client's feeling, because they are 'stuck'. Introducing the metaphor might be a way for them to work with something outside the pain of their grief. So you might say to them:

> 'We've been meeting now for a few sessions, and I'm wondering where you think you are now. Perhaps if we talk about your "grief journey", we might give it a name, so that we create a word picture. What word picture might you use to best describe your journey?'

If they don't readily grasp what you mean, you might say:

> 'Can I help you out here and make some suggestions? Would you say it's like being on a rollercoaster…or a road…or like being in a river…or on a railway track? … Perhaps you might have your own word picture for it?'

Give them time to digest what is needed and you might have a few false starts but it is hoped they will get the idea that you are working with word pictures. Depending on the metaphor they choose to use, you might be able to identify for them that it feels to you as if they are in a 'lay-by', or caught up 'at the bank', or stopped off 'at a station', something that represents the idea of being stuck. They might be able to pick up on that and explain what is going on for them. I have persevered with people who have been stuck, and who struggled with this concept, but it has proved to be helpful in getting them going again. This is another way of accompanying them on the journey, and if they take to the idea of the metaphor, you can use it as a reference point for them in future sessions.

Another way of using the element is towards the end of the time of visiting with someone. It is the kind of subject you may discuss when you know that the session is leading up to or is going to be the last time you see them. You have gone on a journey yourselves in the bereavement sessions if you have heard their stories; you have explored their relationship; you have validated and appreciated the life and discovered the legacies; and you have affirmed or challenged their strategies. There is then a natural progression towards thinking about a journey.

WHAT QUESTIONS CAN YOU ASK?

As you have seen from the above, there are many questions you can ask once you have got them to think of the concept of working with a metaphor, or word picture, to describe their journey. So I shall only add a few more to the ones I have already suggested.

Some questions to get you started:

> What word picture would you give to describe the journey you've been on?

> If I gave you the pictures of a rollercoaster, or a long winding road, or a river, which one would you say describes your grief journey best?

> If you were to describe the place you're in now, what would it look like, using a word picture?

> How does this journey of grief compare with other journeys in your life?

> What is the worst part of this journey for you?

> Who is with you on this journey?

> Where is your loved one on this journey?

In a review or at the end of your visits you could use these questions:

> How is this place different from where you were six months ago (whatever the time frame is)?

> What would you say you are doing differently to what you were doing three months ago (again whatever the time frame is)?

> What major things have you found out about yourself on this journey?

WHAT TECHNIQUES CAN YOU USE?

Life line. Ask them to draw out their own life line.

It will be important for you to have had experience of this yourself, so pause now and reflect on your own losses and your own life. What has the journey been like? Where have you been physically, geographically, emotionally, job-wise, relationally, spiritually? What have been some of the losses you've experienced: jobs, houses, places, relationships?

I would encourage you to do the paper and pen exercise that I described in Chapter 1. Try to record the events chronologically, as this will show you how you went from one event or time of life to another. It may be useful to talk it over with a friend or someone from your peer group that will listen to you. If you are part of a bereavement or pastoral team it might be good to do it as part of your 'experiential work'. When I have done this with nurses and carers on the courses I teach, I find them really surprised at how they have gained a perspective from looking at their lives in this way and then talking about their experiences. They do this for only a few minutes together but they tell me, without fail, that it is a powerful exercise for them.

If you have managed to do your own you will have an experience that will be very helpful for the client's understanding, and you will be able to give them some guidance from seeing what patterns can emerge.

Draw out (or write out) the journey of grief. Use this only with those you know that would be able to cope with this task. Ask: 'Would you be able to draw out the experience of your grief journey so far…the rollercoaster (the road, the river, rail track and so on)?' If you have large paper and felt tip pens they can begin it in the session with you and may want to carry on afterwards. However, for those who are good with words, they may wish to write out their experience as they have thought about it with you. For those who are creative, it can be a very therapeutic exercise.

Collage work: I have worked with some creative clients who have used magazines to cut out words and pictures they have then used to depict their journey, using symbols as well to add to the meaning. The explanations of these can prove to be fruitful and help you to ask questions that might not have arisen before.

IMPACT ON YOU AS A LISTENER

This can be one of the most challenging and most interactive of the elements, as it requires your most 'immediate' involvement. By that, I mean you may need to be thinking in a creative way about the meta-phors the client is using and how you interact with them in the 'here and now' of the session, so as not to lose the opportunity you have been given. Of course, you can always refer back to the metaphors in a later session and say that you have been thinking about what they have said and you wondered if you could explore it again with them.

One of the things I have to be aware of, because I really enjoy working with metaphors, is that I do not take the metaphor too far away from the person's experience and get into a picture that is not theirs. I also have to be careful not to read too much into their responses and lead them into areas that are not relevant for them. If you find yourself having the same problem, check out with the client that they have understood, and that what is being described is actually true for them. I ask for an example from them to clarify it. If I find myself getting carried away and it is my voice I can hear, then I know I have got to get back to listening to their voice. There can be these detours along the way for us and being aware of our own tendencies can be helpful in correcting them.

This might feel like a strange and new element, a little like the element of finding out about the legacies left behind. When we try something new, it feels strange at first until we develop our own ways of working with it, and I would most sincerely encourage you to do that with this element. Perhaps in your supervision sessions or training sessions, you can practise using the metaphor with each other in talking about your own journeys.

In summary:

- We have considered how the 'phases' (Parkes) and the 'tasks of mourning' (Worden) both seem to cover four steps along the journey, and how the experience of our team has generally matched what they have concluded.

- The normal journey that bereaved people are on seems to go round in circles rather than in a straight line, with a lot of movement backwards and forwards between certain behaviours.

- Some of the metaphors that can be used to describe the journey are: the rollercoaster; the river; the long and winding road; the railway track; the tidal ebb and flow; the whirlpool (the quicksand, the earthquake or tsunami, the maze).

- The listening activity is to chart the client's pathway and accompany them on their way.

- Use the element of the journey at times of review; or when you feel the client is stuck; or when you come to deciding how many more sessions to plan in; and in your final session.

CHAPTER 7

There are difficult issues to explore

Unhappily, many people who receive support after a death may not find the experience as helpful as we think. Some people have found that they have not been able to talk about the one who died; that the relationship with the deceased was not explored; that their culture and their belief systems were not taken into account; or that subjects such as finance, work, sex, the impact of friends and society in general were not covered. People want to talk about the one who died and sometimes to talk about the presence of their loved one which they feel helps maintain the close bond, or simply brings comfort at times of low emotional depths. I make these statements based on the research done by a bereavement counsellor, Sally Flatteau Taylor (2005), who in her MA study interviewed ten people about their experience of counselling following bereavement. She reports that some felt they were directed away from what they wanted to talk about by the counsellor who was using a particular theory; another counsellor did not empathize with the client who could feel the presence of her dead husband. It would seem that even for experienced counsellors, there are issues that appear difficult to discuss. I propose to write briefly about three difficult issues we might wish to avoid but which might be necessary to confront at some level: sexuality, spirituality and self harm or suicidal thoughts. I hope to be able to show how we might address them when talking sensitively with bereaved people.

Pause to reflect, again with pen and paper if you wish, about the issues and words that come to mind when you think about the subject of sexuality with bereaved people in mind.

SEXUALITY

I took advantage of having a bereavement team who could work on this with me in some of our training sessions. Some of the words they came up with were:

> relationship, love, physical needs, wants, desire, physical expression, affection, hugs, lust, sex drive, pain, pleasure, fertility, closeness, isolation, loneliness, guilt, identity, same sex relationships, gender, femininity, masculinity, intimacy, power, role changes, potency, lesbian, gay.

I wonder how many of those corresponded with your list. I am hazarding a guess that if I were to ask you which ones of the above might you feel uncomfortable talking about with a client, you might be able to identify something that is personal to you. When faced with a bereaved person, particularly with the one who has lost a partner or spouse, would you feel comfortable talking about their need for intimacy and what they are now doing with their sexual desires? Well, I guess it wouldn't be the first thing on your agenda in your sessions. It wasn't high on ours, either.

I asked my team, 'So, what gets in the way of talking about this issue, for us and the client?' The first thing they talked about was embarrassment – the client's and ours. As a stranger moving into someone's life and having the privilege of hearing about their emotional struggles and pains, it feels too base, somehow, too lewd to start thinking and talking about sex. Perhaps the client does not want to talk about their struggle in this area either, even though it might be a real struggle and a problem. This means, of course, there is avoidance on both sides. No one wants to talk about it – so it is not addressed. This is acceptable if the client is happy enough not to talk about this subject, whether it has to do with what happened before the death or whether it is about what is going on now for them. My concern is that they might wish to talk about it and there has been no opportunity opened up for them to do so. They may have taken their cue from us – we don't want to go into that difficult place with them. Some of the team were concerned about the client's privacy and they had a fear of intruding, and of course this is a good thing to keep in mind, so we do not go blundering in without due care and attention to their sensitivity. However, there might be some clues they give us, and some discreet ways of addressing the issue so as to avoid invading their privacy. Others had a fear of appearing voyeuristic, and the subject might open things up that would be better not spoken about. This helped others think about their own vulnerability – if a woman was seeing a male client and the subject came up, they might feel uncomfortable about their own space and safety. What if talking about this gave the wrong idea and impression of them to the client? These are real issues, as we do have to be careful to safeguard ourselves in these vulnerable places with vulnerable people. Some of the women on the team do not feel comfortable seeing a male client in his house on their own, and some of the men on the team do not feel comfortable meeting a female client at their home, especially in the evening. These issues are easily addressed if we talk about them honestly, so that they are not asked to take on a client where they might feel compromised. It has happened that an older client began to display some inappropriate behaviour towards a female support worker and in supervision we had to help her think about how she might be able to address this with him and to help him with the disappointment and any embarrassment he might also have felt.

The bereavement team also wondered if age could be influencing them and their clients in not allowing them to address the issue of sexuality. We do not know for sure but there was some conjecture about whether or not the younger people are, the more open they are to this kind of discussion, and perhaps older people might feel less inclined to talk openly. We also considered if the way someone presents to you when you are listening to them might prevent you from taking the risk of going into this area; a forbidding demeanour or attitude could be quite inhibiting. Some of the team were also concerned that we did not want to risk shocking our clients and therefore affecting the good relationship that had already been established.

I would never suggest you talk about this subject if you thought you might be placed in a difficult or vulnerable position with your client. In that event, however, you would need to discuss the client at supervision, because there may be other issues going on that need to be attended to.

So, let's look at some ways you might be able to deal with the subject if it did come up. There might be some clues from the client that might tentatively move you towards a discussion about their sexuality.

The client has said, 'During the last months (of the illness) I moved out of the double bed into the spare room.'

What might you think of saying in response? Just try to imagine what might have been going on for them as a couple. You can't make any assumptions that the client is talking about having a good night's sleep. There might have been a number of reasons for this move, some could be practical. Perhaps the incontinency of the partner, perhaps the sight, sounds and smells became too much. Perhaps something else was going on for them in their relationship. You do need to be tentative in your response:

> *Support worker*: You felt you needed to move out. I wonder if you might feel comfortable talking a bit more about that?

In this way you have not presumed to move into any area without the willingness of the client to do so. If the subject is about sexuality you will need to go carefully and check out that the client is still agreeable to talk about this. The client may head you off anyway and say that they do not want to talk about it; at least you will have provided the opportunity.

The client says, 'He became distant and stopped speaking.'

This is a little more open; something had happened, perhaps it could have been between them, or it could have been due to his fear of dying, or his way of coping with the stress, and many more reasons. Whatever it was, she has been affected by this as she has remembered it clearly.

> *Support worker*: He seemed to shut himself off from you. How did you cope with that?

You could go on at some point to say:

> *Support worker*: You might have missed the intimacies of your relationship too, if he'd closed down.

If she wants to carry on with that discussion about 'intimacies', she will follow your tentative lead. If not, she will move onto another subject.

The client has said, 'I wasn't able to show any affection to him.'

Maybe there was something wrong for her that she could not show affection, or about him that prevented her; you do not know until she tells you more. What you can do is reflect what she was struggling with.

> *Support worker:* It became difficult for you to show your normal ways of being affectionate with him.

This may help her to agree and tell you about what it was, or she may correct you and tell you what was going on that prevented her. Again, you could go on to talk about the loss of intimacy and closeness that resulted.

The client says, 'We became like strangers.'

What might have happened to bring this about? Sadness pervades this statement, and without knowing too much you can only surmise that once they were close and then at some point they weren't.

> *Support worker:* It seems you lost the closeness that you'd once had in your relationship.

If they had not been close, she will tell you, but if they had she will possibly share what it used to be like. Possibly she might be feeling the rejection at the end of their relationship and is left wondering what it was all about, as she had lost something precious even before he died.

The client says, 'Things weren't so good between the two of us.'

This is quite an admission, as it feels loaded with all sorts of issues, one of which might be about their sexual relationship.

> *Support worker:* You say things weren't good between the two of you; I wonder if you might want to say more about that.

That is the invitation for the client to disclose or not.

Although these statements in themselves might not appear to be about sexuality, they are statements about the relationship, which might lead you towards a discussion of something of that nature, so you should not ignore these kinds of remarks.

Looking at photographs might provide the opportunity to talk about changes in appearance and how that might have affected their relationship. The client might go into details about the appearance of the deceased (looking older, more haggard), the weight changes (thinner or fatter), skin textures, pain areas, fear of hurting.

Here are some possible open questions for you to make:

'What kind of changes did you have to face in your relationship?'

'What kind of tensions did you experience in your intimacy? (Your desire for each other? Your sharing? Your moods? Your closeness?)'

'Perhaps it's hard to talk about some issues with your family, for instance how you might be missing the physical closeness with your wife.'

'Some people have spoken about having problems with their sex life during the time of the illness. I wonder if that might have happened to you?'

You will notice that the questions above got bolder as we have progressed, and I think that is the natural progression for us to make in this area. I would strongly suggest that these questions be used with clients you have known for some time and have a strong suspicion that they might want to talk about this topic.

On the other hand there are clients who are explicit in their need to talk about this issue. Here are some things that you might hear. I have given some responses, which use the reflective listening skill so that you can see it is not too difficult to stay with the client, even when they are talking about a sensitive topic.

Client: I miss the presence of my wife in bed.

Support worker: You miss the closeness and physical intimacy you had with your wife.

Client: I struggled with my sexual desire before she died.

Support worker: You found it hard to deal with your desire for normal sexual activity while she was ill.

Client: I knew we would never have sex again.

Support worker: You knew this was the end of your sexual relationship with her.

Client: I feel embarrassed talking about my sexual desire now.

Support worker: You feel embarrassed to talk about such intimate things as your sexual desire. And yet you've raised it, so I wonder if you want to continue to talk about it. It seems like something that is a concern to you.

These responses may seem ridiculous on paper, but in the real conversation, they are encouraging and helpful to the client who is probably testing out what they can say or not say. Furthermore, they are probably testing out how you will respond. Will you respond by avoiding the matter altogether and moving on to something else? Will you react with shock? Or will you be accepting of what they say, so that they can go on? By the way, silence at this point will be seen as avoidance. If they drop these statements into the conversation and rush on themselves, you can always come back to it, by saying something like:

'I wonder if I could come back to something you said just now about missing the presence of your wife in bed. It sounds as if you miss the closeness and physical intimacy with your wife.'

Please don't go away after reading this chapter and see something sexual in every conversation you have with a bereaved person; it won't be there necessarily. But being aware of what you can say and how to respond might make it easier for you to go into more depth. Let me give you encouragement from the experience of one of our male support workers. He was surprised when he gently responded in something like the above way when visiting a client whose sexual life was of real concern. Because the support worker didn't opt out but followed what the client was saying sensitively, the client was able to explore the struggle he was having, and it eventually worked out well for him. The support worker was really pleased that he hadn't backed away from such a sensitive issue, and was satisfied that the outcome was of help to his client. What's more, he hadn't given his client a single word of advice. The skills you need are not counselling skills. You need to master the art of reflecting so that you stay with the client and so that you don't take the lead. With this subject it is vital you don't direct the client where you think they should be going. Let them dictate the pace and the depth.

SPIRITUALITY

Now to address another issue that gets avoided in some bereavement conversations, and again, like the issue of sexuality, you do not have to go hunting for this, but you do need to be aware that there could be issues around the spiritual life of the client that could at least be acknowledged in your discussions. Spirituality is a little bit like an umbrella term, I think, for those areas of our lives that seem inexplicable. These areas are neither just emotional, nor just physical and not wholly rational but something else that is going on for the person. I am aware too that from my experience with bereaved clients they would say that being religious is not necessarily the same as being spiritual but that being spiritual may lead to something religious. Because this is such a profoundly difficult subject area, I will not be able to do it justice, but I do want to include something on it because sometimes these issues are around for people.

There may be those who count themselves as religious because of their affiliation with a church, synagogue, temple or mosque and would welcome the opportunity to speak about their faith system in relation to the way they are coping. When we see people in their bereaved state they may be vulnerable and in need of some spiritual support. They may have had a faith, but through the experiences their faith is now rocked and they feel angry towards God. They can't reconcile what they've always believed with what they've witnessed and experienced. In this instance the question may arise, 'How can a loving God allow suffering in this world – and especially to my loved one, who was a good person?' (I have given a possible response to this below.) On the other hand there are people who have never had a faith of any description who at this time find themselves questioning and seeking for answers about the greater purpose in life. For them it is a life changing experience and they are led to a faith in God. A Sikh woman shared with me how she hadn't really taken her faith seriously before her husband died, and afterwards she was livid with God. This lasted a few months and then she began to go back to the temple and had found a new faith.

People may find comfort in their religious beliefs, and church or temple life may become quite important to them. Certain rituals may become very important to people; for example, the mourning traditions of a culture may bring great relief and comfort because they provide structure and people know what they are to do. They have a role to play and there are expected things to be done, at a time perhaps when life seems without purpose and the structures that were in place before are no longer there.

We need to meet people where they are with respect for their choices and their own beliefs or none. It may be through your compassionate and sensitive communication with them in this area that they begin to make their own exploration of a spiritual pathway. It should not be our goal to lead them in any particular spiritual or religious journey (we would not wish to be accused of exploiting vulnerable people). Talking about their struggles in an appropriate way might, however, allow them the freedom to express what might be otherwise left unexpressed. With the adverse press some people have received for going into spiritual areas, we can become a little paranoid about the boundaries around spiritual care. By adopting the approach I am suggesting, I do not think anyone would be able to accuse you of overstepping the boundaries.

Our work with people is in supporting them in a holistic way, which may include spiritual support. Some of those spiritual needs might show themselves in the need to know the deceased is at peace, or safe and well, free of pain. They are looking for reassurance about the departed spirit of their loved one. People are often looking for answers to such questions as:

Why did it happen to (their loved one)? Why did it happen to me? How can I go on without her? Will I meet her again? Why did he have to suffer? Where was God in this? What purpose does life have?

We can not answer these questions; there are no answers that would suffice in these circumstances. If we try to enter into a theological discussion, there may be a genuine chance of offending and of alienating the person you want to support. We do not say, 'Well, what I believe is…' You might think this is acceptable; after all, you're only giving your own ideas. However, it just might be that very remark that offends them and you will not see them again. What you can do, however, is reflect back to them what they are struggling with:

> *Support worker:* You really seem to be struggling with some of the big issues of life, about the suffering of human beings, and particularly your wife, and the place of God in it all.

This might be enough to start them thinking aloud or it may be enough that their struggle was acknowledged. Sometimes, all your client wants from you is that you have heard and understood where they are coming from – without having the answers.

You might want to think about how you can enable people to talk about their 'spiritual' experiences. Talking about the presence of the person is frequently heard and we do not shy away from it. What is important to find out is how the presence, the dream, or the vision impacted on the client. Of course, there are those who have been told by a well-meaning friend or relative to expect the presence of the loved one to return. They wait, but nothing happens. Your sensitivity is needed here in not dismissing their longing for the presence of their loved one to appear:

> *Support worker.* You've been waiting for her presence to come to you and it seems very hard that nothing's happened. What are you struggling with most as you wait?

You will need to help them deal with the huge sense of rejection and disappointment they might feel, which can be like a double bereavement.

> *Support worker.* It seems that you set a lot of store by what your friend said, and now you're having to rethink what's going on. On the one hand it seems you're disappointed nothing's happened, and on the other, you feel she's gone from you for ever.

Sometimes you have to reflect back the hard things that you hear in the words they are using, so that they can hear their own thoughts and emotions about a subject.

If they have experienced a sense of the presence of the deceased, some will say they find such an experience comforting; others will be concerned and distressed by such things, particularly waking up from a dream to the reality of the empty bed.

Let's have a look at some examples of what people might say to you and some ideas of how to respond.

The client says, 'I felt his presence last night. I could feel the weight of his hand on my shoulder the way he used to do when passing my chair. I looked round because I thought he was there.'

You want to show respect for this experience and not dismiss it, but you want to focus on the impact on the client rather than sensationalizing the event:

> *Support worker:* You were so certain he had touched you that you looked for him. How did that affect you?

You might go on to explore other times she had experienced such things, and also to ask her what she makes of these experiences. Maybe she doesn't make anything of them, but accepts them and welcomes them. In telling you she perhaps wants you to validate her experience. On the other hand, it may be that she does believe that this is a sign from the other side and you can explore that with her. Remember, these are their experiences, not yours. You do not have to agree with them, only explore the impact the experience has on them.

Someone tells you, 'I've had dreams about her. They seem so real, as if she's trying to communicate with me from the other side. Do you think I'm crazy?'

Regardless of what you might believe about dreams and the spirit world, you need to be sensitive to this man's concerns.

> *Support worker:* Your dreams of her have made you wonder if she's trying to tell you something – or talk to you. I wonder how you're left feeling afterwards.

Here you can explore if the dreams were comforting to the client or not. If they left him feeling distressed, what was he concerned about? Maybe he was troubled that her spirit is not settled and she is going to be a restless soul. Maybe he thinks there is some secret she wants to communicate with him about. Explore this issue with sensitive questions:

> *Support worker:* What are your biggest fears (concerns/worries) about this?

It might be important just to ask if he wants to tell you what he sees in the dreams. A client who had vivid dreams wanted to tell me about them in minute detail, as if rehearsing them so she wouldn't forget them. I expressed this thought, and she agreed this was what she was doing. She'd found the dreams vaguely distressing but strangely comforting too. I suggested she could try writing them down in detail, and because she was quite an artistic woman I wondered if she might want to paint or write them into a poem or song. She did choose to write them down and the dreams stopped. She had the memories written down and could go back to visit them again if she chose. Because I had entered into that spiritual space with her, she realized that I didn't think she was strange, even though I hadn't said as much to her.

More and more we are coming into contact with people who are attending spiritualist churches or clairvoyants in order to be in touch with their loved ones. This may or not be disconcerting to you, and asking a gentle question might be helpful, like:

'How did you find that experience?' Or,

'What feelings or thoughts were you left with afterwards?'

They sometimes want to find out what you think about this kind of spiritual experience. I have learnt to answer this with something that I feel is honest:

'I think it's more important to find out what you think about it. What did you want from the experience and did you get what you wanted?'

We can help people explore what they want and what they are looking for, and if they find it in these ways, then we can help them decide if they will continue seeking in this way or not.

It might be that after some discussion with the client you feel they could benefit from support from a chaplain, a vicar or minister and it might be helpful to find out who they might trust or respect. Sometimes they have had good contact with the vicar or minister who conducted the funeral service and this might be a person they could talk to. It is always wise to know how far you can personally go. If you feel the client wants to have those hard discussions about life and death which make you uncomfortable, or you feel you should keep the boundaries around your own work, then encourage the client to seek appropriate support in this area. They may still wish to keep talking to you, of course, and if you are comfortable with that, go ahead. But be sure to tell them that you will not be talking with them about the discussions they have with the vicar or minister, as you could be cast into the role of a referee.

You may be wondering why I have not said very much about the different cultural or religious contexts you might operate in. In working with this approach, which we have done for several years now, we have seen many people from a variety of different cultural and religious backgrounds and we have seen the approach work across the board. We have been able to listen to the stories that are set in different contexts, and explore the relationships within those contexts too. We have found that the clients we have seen from different cultural and religious backgrounds tell us about their traditions and their ways of doing things quite willingly. They will also tell us when they do not wish to conform to those norms. The approach works for us in a positive way for all the clients we have seen regardless of their cultural, religious or sexual orientations.

Finally, on this aspect of bereavement conversations my encouragement is not to be afraid of spiritual issues. If they come up, reflect back to the client what has happened for them and explore with them what it means to them. Remember, you are not going to have the answers that they want anyway, and you can not fix people's pain and struggles. It just might be that they have to wrestle with these existential questions of life in order to find out what they really believe.

SELF HARM OR SUICIDAL THOUGHTS

Before we look at this subject you might want to reflect on your own concerns about encountering someone who might talk to you about suicidal thoughts or actions of a self-harming nature.

As a bereavement team, we had our discussions before we moved towards establishing some guidelines for working with clients who were vulnerable in this way. The team had some concerns which I will share with you here. One of their concerns was about missing the signs that would indicate someone felt suicidal; some were also worried that they would not know the signs because of a lack of personal experience or knowledge in this area. There was a concern for some in not knowing what to do if the client started to talk seriously about considering suicide. They were especially concerned about what to do if the client threatened they were going to do something after the session. Some admitted honestly that they might not have taken the client's threats seriously enough. On a personal level, there might also be the concern about feeling the desolation for the client, and a fear of getting sucked in, or becoming tearful and so being unhelpful in the situation.

Finding the person after they had made an attempt was another concern, in the way it would not only impact them but what to do in such an event. Supposing they had got in through the front door – what then? There was alarm at the thought of the publicity and the stigma attached in the event of a suicide, not only for the client but for themselves. There would also be the aftermath of berating themselves with 'If only I'd done this' or 'If only I'd said that.' We thought we might also need to face anger, on several fronts: of those left behind who might be angry with us for not having done more; the anger against the deceased relative; and also coming to terms with our own anger against the client. These are real fears and concerns.

We recognize that in working with bereaved people there is a risk of a client seriously considering suicide. We also recognize that many clients may perceive life as not worth living and they feel they can't go on without their loved one, telling us that they want to be with their loved one. They may communicate this to a counsellor or support worker, a church worker, nurse or friend while in no way actively considering ending their lives. As support workers we know that there are times when we will hear clients say things like, 'I can't go on without her. But I know I won't do anything.'

I will take space here to reflect on some of the factors that might place bereaved people at risk of suicidal thoughts and plans. Some of these factors are: isolation and loneliness; depression; stress; multiple losses; poor health issues; not wanting to be a burden; extreme situations of financial worry and debt; family conflicts; loss of purpose in life; having no hope for the future; previous mental ill health. It is often not just one of those factors, but a number together that usually cause someone to attempt suicide. It is difficult to say whether someone is going to do something harmful to themselves, but there may be ways of helping us assess a situation. We bear in mind that there will be a large number of bereaved individuals who may feel suicidal but have no intention of acting on these feelings. What we need to do then is assess the level of risk and imminence. Are they going to do something to take their lives imminently, or as soon as you leave the house, or during the coming days? This level of imminence should be what affects the way you decide to act. The question is whether or not they are likely to act on their thoughts and impulses.

What stops us immediately phoning the police or ambulance or doctor when we suspect someone's intention is to harm themselves? For us in the caring professions it is about the issue of confidentiality. We want to respect the confidentiality of the relationship and also the client's rights to their own choices. Some people will say, 'If that's what they want to do they must be allowed to do it. It's about their autonomy.' We need to balance this right to autonomy with the duty of care we have towards the client. So there may be instances where it will be appropriate to break that confidentiality for the client's sake.

It is vital that you talk to your clients about this in the setting up and 'contracting' stage at the first session where you are preparing the client for what you are going to offer and what you are not offering. Before all this gets to feel too big and dangerous or even bureaucratic, let me suggest that in your initial session, you can say something like:

> 'I'm hoping it won't happen, but it's better to be clear about this. It may become necessary for me to break confidentiality at some point should there be any cause for concern about your safety, or about doing any harm to yourself or anybody else. And if there is ever a time, I would be talking to you about it.'

It may be that some clients will be quite open about their thoughts at this point. I have had clients who will say, 'Well, actually, I've had thoughts about this and I do still feel a bit like it at the moment.' I address how to respond to this further on.

Some clients may not be able to express suicidal feelings whether implicitly or explicitly. Some individuals will make explicit references to suicide. However, it is possible that suicidal thoughts may lie behind some statements, such as, 'I can't see the point any more.' Or, 'It would be better if I weren't here any more.' So we do need to follow up statements like this. You might hear other things, like, 'I don't know why I'm going on.' 'It all seems just too hard at the moment.' 'I just want to be with her.' 'Life has no meaning or purpose now.' 'I don't want to wake up in the mornings.'

Here are some suggestions about how you can respond to those bleak pronouncements:

> 'These seem to be quite dark thoughts you're having. Have you talked about how you feel with any one else?'

> 'You seem to be saying you've lost purpose in life. Has it been so bad that you've thought of taking your own life?'

> 'I wonder if you've given up on life. Have you ever thought seriously about suicide?'

If they answer that they have had thoughts about suicide or self harm, then you ask:

> 'Have you ever thought of how and when you might do this? Have you any plans?'

If in following this line of discussion, you feel some concern for your client's safety, but it does not appear to be imminent, there are some things you can do. You should gently tell the client of your concerns and discuss with them the best course of action. It is necessary to explore certain things with them. In the first instance, discuss with them what family and social support they could involve in their lives to help them through this time. It might mean strongly encouraging the client to seek help from their doctor, or another appropriate support agency. As an extra support it might be an idea to carry the number of your local Samaritan service or emergency help line for them to use at times of stress. This has the advantage that it is a 24 hour service. It may be appropriate to check with them whether or not they have a stock of drugs in the house which could be disposed of while you are there, if they are willing to do so. Seek advice from your bereavement service manager on all of these issues.

You should always discuss an active risk of suicide with your supervisor, and tell the client that you are doing so. At the hospice when this has happened, I make sure I call the client and make a visit to talk about the way the client is feeling. This helps the bereavement team feel safe and they have the support of a qualified member of staff who is then going to do the risk assessment. Should the risk to your client be urgent, and you feel that the client is at risk of committing suicide after you leave, you should follow the policy guidelines your organization has in place. However, if your organization does not already have a policy in place for you to follow, here are a few suggested guidelines:

> You should stay with the client, explaining that this is your duty of care. Ask them to give you a contact number of a family member or friend that they would like to ask to come round immediately. Ask them to make that call, or ask permission to do it on their behalf.
>
> Contact their doctor, or if you can't raise a doctor, contact the local out of hours social service team and talk to them about what to do.
>
> Make sure someone in your own family or someone at your office knows you are being delayed and if it is at all possible, contact your supervisor.
>
> If a client tells you they have just taken an overdose of pills, with or without alcohol, I advise that you alert the emergency services immediately and put the above into operation.

If suicide is not immediately threatened but you are unsure about the client's intentions, you should take the issue to supervision, either immediately over the phone or as soon as possible. Ensure that you make notes of all that you did and said so that you can show you took as much care as you could and were not negligent in your duty of care.

If in reading this you feel daunted by the discussion, please remember that, in the majority of cases, most people will tell you they have no plan to do anything to themselves and are expressing their longing to see their loved one again.

IMPACT ON YOU AS A LISTENER

It is always deeply impacting to consider that someone you have worked with is contemplating taking their own lives. You need support through this. If in the sad event a client does commit or attempt suicide, it is important to remember that the best care in the world will not prevent some people killing themselves. You should avail yourself of support from your supervisor and your peer group if you have one. If there is a counsellor available in your service or organization, it might be worthwhile having a session or two with them to talk over the impact this has had on you. It is deeply troubling and upsetting to be part of an attempted or actual suicide, but if you seek support you will have a good chance of being able to work it through and to return to bereavement support work with some experience that will help you and others in the future. Of course, you should remember that you only share any details of this with authorized people and that agreements about confidentiality continue beyond the client's death.

I would strongly urge you to work with your organization, church or society to come up with some protocols or procedures for working with bereaved people who are suicidal. Being prepared by having some training might prove to be invaluable. Thinking this through for yourself will mean you are more able to resolve some of the ethical dilemmas in a considered manner. By not avoiding the difficult issues, some of your clients will be helped to talk through their darker moments, knowing they are not 'off limits'.

We have a set of guidelines and protocols at the hospice that have arisen out of the team's training sessions and it has helped us to feel less insecure and more able to operate responsibly if and when anything should happen to one of our clients. If your organization does not have a policy in place for you to follow, it would be advantageous to ask other organizations who operate in similar ways if they would allow you sight of their policies. Most charitable organizations are more than willing to assist with these requests.

Conclusion

In coming to the end of this process, I am aware of some themes that have emerged and some issues that need underlining. First, the relationship with the bereaved person is the most significant help to them. This relationship, however, needs to be grounded in good active listening, empathic exploration and a willingness to talk about the hard issues that the bereaved person is dealing with. I believe those who wish to support bereaved people should become skilled particularly in the listening skills and in learning about some of the contemporary thinking around bereavement. As you will have noted, I have been particularly encouraged and informed by the writings of Robert Neimeyer and Thomas Attig and I would recommend you try to read some of their work. But I hope you will be interested enough, from the brief synopses of some of the other theories and models I have used, to read them for yourselves.

Second, supervision is vital for you to have when you are dealing with people whose sorrows are considerable, the weight of which can sit heavily on your shoulders or in your heart. Many times members of the bereavement team tell me that the best thing about a supervision session is that they can talk through the pain and struggles they have listened to with their clients. If you do not belong to an organization that offers you supervision, I would consider trying to obtain it for yourself through another organization that does offer supervision in bereavement work, and paying for it if necessary.

Third, I would like to underline the importance of having experiential practice of the techniques in the tool box before you work with a client in these ways. I truly believe that it is important that you understand their impact on you so that you will feel comfortable and at ease with them when you use them with a client. Fourth, the theme of referring onto other professionals has emerged. You may have become aware that there will be some people you see who might be in need of help that is outside what you can offer. There will be people who are experiencing more complicated grief than you can deal with, so it would be my suggestion that you operate with some humility in this and not try to take on more than you are qualified to do. If in any doubt about someone's well-being and mental health, be sure to discuss it with your supervisor and have the addresses and contact numbers of your local agencies to contact.

Fifth, I would like to reiterate that no matter how much we listen and how good we are at entering into the world of another, people still have to bear their own pain. We can not dispense a tablet for emotional pain relief, though I acknowledge some may need the assistance of antidepressants. There is no magic formula and no magic wand to wave. People will still experience the pain and sorrow of loss, and this is probably as it should be. So we should not try to rescue them or solve their pain or fix it for them. If they have the ability at some point in their lives to experience even a glimpse of joy again, and yet carry the loss with them, then perhaps we will have supported them well. There is a way of looking at some people's grief and acknowledging that they might be in 'chronic sorrow'. Sorrow that goes on for a long time, without totally disabling the person, where the pain of loss is felt just as deeply as at the beginning and yet where the bereaved person does not live in total despair, may be sorrow that can be called 'chronic'. Ted Bowman (2007) writes: 'It seems that as long as bereaved people are able to function well with daily tasks and can experience beauty in life, the presence of chronic sorrow could be understood, acknowledged, even supported as an acceptable way of grieving' (p.49).

You may encounter someone who does not want to talk and feels your sessions are a waste of time. I believe you will be able to engage even this person at some level with this approach. It will be important anyway to be honest with the person who appears to be resistant, and say something like:

'I get the general impression that it is really difficult for you to talk about your grief. I wonder if this is the right time for you or would it be better left until you feel more able to share?'

On a personal note, as I began writing this book, my mother died. As I have been completing it a young member of my husband's family died suddenly and tragically. We were thrown into the middle of shock, disbelief and pain, our own and that of my husband's family. We had many conversations with them. If the approach I have presented here was to be credible then I needed it to help me in these conversations. I sat and listened to the stories, especially the agonizing and painful stories around his death, which will continue to be picked over for a long time ahead. We talked about what the young man meant to his parents, his sister, to us and to his friends. We celebrated many of his achievements, recalling his talented short life and what he had achieved and how he had helped others in his wide circle of friends. I needed to let them share their pain and, in this instance, let them hear mine too. The approach did help me.

We find the stories our client tells of their loved one's life are at the heart of the best conversations. As you move into the heart of their sorrow, you can bring a sense of meaning. I consider that listening to a bereaved client is a privilege; they let me into deep parts of their heart and their life, and I marvel at the courage many show in the face of profound sorrow. Many of these people have been examples for me and witnesses of what it means to live with a broken heart but still to love others and be part of their 'relearned' world. Let me give Thomas Attig the last word: 'Grieving is a journey of the heart that brings us to the fullness of life in the flesh and blood, here and now, and into the future with those who still share the earth with us' (2001, p.52).

Appendix: An overview of the six elements

	Element	Listening activity	Questions	Techniques in your tool box	Theory
1.	There is a story	Hear it and assist them to construct a bigger picture	Tell me about… (name) What sort of person was he? How did you meet? What did he like doing, as hobbies or interests?	Photographs Three memory stones Memory jars, life-story books and memory boxes Draw/write a biographical life line Journals, letters	Biography: T. Walter Meaning Reconstruction: R. Neimeyer T. Attig
2.	There is a relationship	Explore it to bring out meaning	What sort of things did he do that made you smile? What kind of things did you do together? In what ways would you say you were different? What have friends said about her?	Draw the family tree Read/write poems, journals, prayers, letters and cards Unsent letter Buttons and stones	Continuing bonds: Stroebe et al.

#					
3.	There is a life to celebrate	Identify the reasons for celebration and validate the significance of them	What were some of the things that she felt were important in life? What were some of the best achievements he was proud of?	Photographs Memory jar: about the achievements of the deceased	Biography Meaning Reconstruction
4.	There is a legacy left behind	Discover it to encourage them in giving worth to the life	What sayings or mannerisms do you remember she had? Who in the family is most like him? What can you see that he has left behind for you to enjoy? What ways of thinking do you think she has passed on to her family?	Family legacies Personal legacy exercise Taking on the 'mantle'	Meaning Reconstruction

Table continued

	Element	Listening activity	Questions	Techniques in your tool box	Theory
5.	There is a strategy for coping	Understand and affirm it or challenge it	About self: How have you found you've coped with other problems in your life? About family members: How is their way of grieving? How does their way of grieving impact you?	The 'Blob Tree' diagram 'Bad Day, Good Day' exercise Buttons or stones	Patterns of grieving: T. Martin and K. Doka Dual Process Model: M. Stroebe and H. Schut
6.	There is a journey undertaken	Chart their pathway and accompany them on their journey	From the image of a road or a river or a whirlpool, which one would you say would describe your own experience best? What would you say you are doing differently to what you were doing three months ago?	Draw out the life journey so far – what patterns emerge? (Life line) Draw out the grief journey so far (rollercoaster, road, the river, etc.) Collage work using magazines	Phases of grieving: C.M. Parkes Tasks of mourning: W. Worden

References

Attig, T. (2001) 'Relearning the World: Making and Finding Meanings.' In R.A. Neimeyer (ed) *Meaning Reconstruction and the Experience of Loss.* Washington: American Psychological Association.

Bayliss, J. (2004) *Counselling Skills in Palliative Care.* Salisbury: Quay Books.

Bowman, T. (2007) 'Chronic sorrow and bereavement care.' *Bereavement Care 26*, 3, 47–50.

Crabb, L. (1987) *Understanding People.* Grand Rapids: Zondervan Publishing House.

Flatteau Taylor, S. (2005) 'Between the idea and the reality: a study of the counselling experiences of bereaved people who sense the presence of the deceased.' *Counselling and Psychotherapy Research 5*, 1, 53–61.

Klass, D., Silverman P.R. and Nickman, S.L. (eds) (1996) *Continuing Bonds: New Understandings of Grief.* Philadelphia: Taylor & Francis.

Marshall, S. (2007) 'Bereavement counselling – is it viable?' *Therapy Today 18*, 5, 4–5.

Martin, T. and Doka, K.J. (1999) *Men Don't Cry…Women Do: Transcending Gender Stereotypes of Grief.* Philadelphia: Routledge.

Neimeyer, R.A. (2000) *Lessons of Loss: A Guide to Coping.* Memphis: Center for the Study of Loss and Transition.

Neimeyer, R.A. (2001) 'The Language of Loss: Grief Therapy as a Process of Meaning Reconstruction.' In R.A. Neimeyer (ed) *Meaning Reconstruction and the Experience of Loss.* Washington: American Psychological Association.

New York International Bible Society. (1978) *The Holy Bible.* Sevenoaks, UK: Hodder & Stoughton.

Parkes, C.M. (1998) 'Bereavement in Adult Life.' In C.M. Parkes and A. Markus (eds) *Coping with Loss.* London: Wiley Blackwell.

Romanoff, B.D. (2001) 'Research as Therapy: The Power of Narrative to Effect Change.' In R.A. Neimeyer (ed) *Meaning Reconstruction and the Experience of Loss.* Washington: American Psychological Association.

Stroebe, M., Gergen, M., Gergen, K. and Stroebe, W. (1996) 'Broken Hearts or Broken Bonds?' In D. Klass, P.R. Silverman and S.L. Nickman (eds) *Continuing Bonds.* Philadelphia: Taylor & Francis.

Stroebe, M. and Schut, H. (1999) 'The Dual Process Model of coping with bereavement: rationale and description.' *Death Studies 23*, 3, 197–224.

Walter, T. (1996) 'A new model of grief: bereavement and biography.' *Mortality 1*, 1, 7–25.

Worden, W. (1991) *Grief Counseling and Grief Therapy.* 2nd edition. London: Routledge.

Further reading

DEATH BY SUICIDE

Hewitt, J. (1980) *After Suicide*. Louisville, Kentucky: Westminster John Knox Press

Riches G. and Dawson P. (2000) *An Intimate Loneliness*. Buckingham: Open University Press.

Wertheimer, A. (2001) *A Special Scar* (2nd edition). Hove: Brunner-Routledge.

BEREAVED PARENTS

Tedeschi, R.G. and Galhoun, L.G. (2004) *Helping Bereaved Parents: A Clinician's Guide*. New York: Routledge.

COUNSELLING SKILLS

Frankland, A. and Sanders, P. (1995) *Next Steps in Counselling: A Student's Companion for Certificate and Counselling Skills Courses*. (Reprinted 2006.) Ross-on-Wye, UK: PCCS Books.

Lendrum, S. and Syme, G. (1992) *Gift of Tears – A Practical Approach to Loss and Bereavement Counselling*. London: Routledge.

Sanders, P. (1994) *First Steps in Counselling: A Student's Companion for Basic Introductory Courses*. Ross-on-Wye, UK: PCCS Books.

Tschudin, V. (1996) *Counselling for Loss and Bereavement*. London: Baillière Tindall.

GENERAL READING

Attig, T. (1996) *How We Grieve: Relearning the World*. New York: Oxford University Press.

Attig, T. (2000) *The Heart of Grief: Death and the Search for Meaning*. New York: Oxford University Press.

Humphrey, G. and Zimpfer, D. (1996) *Counselling for Grief and Bereavement* (2nd edition 2008). London: Sage Publishers.

Jeffreys, J.S. (2005) *Helping Grieving People – When Tears Are Not Enough – A Handbook for Care Providers*. New York: Brunner-Routledge.

Roos, S. (2002) *Chronic Sorrow: A Living Loss*. New York: Brunner-Routledge.

Walter, T. (1999) *On Bereavement – The Culture of Grief*. Buckingham: Open University Press.

Weinstein, J. (2008) *Working with Loss, Death and Bereavement: A Guide for Social Workers*. London: Sage.

PRACTICAL AND CREATIVE

Sunderland, M. and Engleheart, P. (1993) *Draw on your Emotions.* (Reprinted 2005.) Oxon, UK: Speechmark.

Wilson, P. and Long, I. (2008) *The Big Book of Blob Trees.* Milton Keynes, UK: Speechmark.

PROFESSIONAL JOURNALS

K. Doka (ed) *Omega: Journal of Death and Dying.* Amityville, NY: Baywood.
[Professional journal drawing on research and insights into attitudes to death, grief, and related issues.]

R.A. Neimeyer (ed) *Death Studies.* Philadelphia: Taylor and Francis.
[Professional journal covering literature in all aspects of death and bereavement.]

C.M. Parkes (ed) *Bereavement Care.* Richmond, UK: Cruse Bereavement Care.
[Articles, reviews and editorials written in non-technical language for those who help bereaved people.]

SPIRITUAL

Ferguson, S.B. (1993) *Deserted by God?* Edinburgh: Banner of Truth Trust.

Frankl, V.E. (1992) *Man's Search for Meaning.* Boston: Beacon Press.

Fraser, L. (1994) *Water from the Rock: Finding Grace in Times of Loss.* New York: Paulist Press.

Useful resources

(All websites accessed 10 February 2009)

Australian Centre for Grief and Bereavement
McCulloch House
Monash Medical Centre
246 Clayton Road
Clayton
VIC 3168
Australia
+61 3 9265 2100
www.grief.org.au

Specialist bereavement service for individuals, children and families.

Bereavement Care Centre
PO Box 835
Wyong
NSW 2259
Australia
+61 2 9804 6909
www.bereavementcare.com.au

Offers complete bereavement care services including bereavement counselling, educational courses, books and DVDs and information for bereaved adults and children in Australia.

British Association for Counselling and Psychotherapy
BACP House
15 St John's Business Park
Lutterworth
Leicestershire LE17 4HB
UK
0870 443 5252
www.bacp.co.uk

Professional association and regulatory body. Information on counselling centres and individual therapists' register. Research and education journals.

Childhood Bereavement Network (CBN)
8 Wakley Street
London EC1V 7QE
020 7843 6309
www.cbn@ncb.org.uk

Information, guidance and support for children, young people and parents.

Child Bereavement Charity
Aston House
West Wycombe
High Wycombe
Bucks HP14 3AG
01494 446648
www.childbereavement.org.uk

Support for bereaved families of a child's death, for young people, schools and professionals.

Compassionate Friends
53 North Street
Bristol BS3 1EN
Helpline: 01173 953 9639
www.tcf.org.uk

Also available – support for siblings:
www.tcfsiblingsupport.org.uk

Supporting bereaved parents and their families. A self-help group for parents who have lost children of any age.

The Compassionate Friends
PO Box 3696
Oak Brook
Illinois 60522-3696
USA
+1 708 990 0010
www.compassionatefriends.org/

An international organization dedicated to supporting the family after a child dies.

Cruse Bereavement Care
PO Box 800
Richmond
Surrey TW9 2RG
0844 477 9400
www.cruse.org.uk

Bereavement support and training.

Hospice Foundation of America
www.hospicefoundation.org/

Resources and advice for anyone coping with death and bereavement in a personal or professional context.

Karnac Bookshop
118 Finchley Road
London NW3 5HT
020 7431 1075
www.karnacbooks.com

Bookseller specializing in psychological therapies.

MIND
15–19 Broadway
London E15 4BQ
Infoline: 0845 766 0163
www.mind.org.uk

Mental health charity. Information, support, counselling, comprehensive information on suicide.

Re.Vision
Centre for Integrative Psychosynthesis Counselling and Psychotherapy
97 Brondesbury Road
London NW6 6RY
020 8357 8881
www.re-vision.org.uk
Therapy training centre and counselling service.

Seesaw
Bush House
2 Merewood Avenue
Headington
Oxford OX3 8EF
01865 744768
www.seesaw.org.uk
Support for bereaved children. A free downloadable resource pack for professionals in schools, and for those supporting children and young people who have a learning difficulty through the experience of bereavement.

Support After Murder or Manslaughter (SAMM)
Crammer House
39 Brixton Road
London SW9 6DZ
020 7735 3838
Helpline: 0845 872 3440
www.samm.org.uk
Information and support for families and friends through mutual support groups.

Stillbirth and Neonatal Death Society (SANDS)
28 Portland Place
London W1N 4DE
Helpline: 020 7436 5881
www.uk-sands.org
Information and support for those affected by the death of a baby and information on research.

Survivors of Bereavement by Suicide (SOBS)
National Office
The Flamsteed Centre
Albert Street
Ilkeston
Derbyshire DE7 5GU
0115 944 1117
National Helpline: 0844 5616855
www.uk-sobs.org.uk

Support for those bereaved by suicide, information, groups and reading material.
Support After a Suicide (2007) is a booklet produced by SOBS.

Terence Higgins Trust
52–54 Gray's Inn Road
London WC1X 8JU
020 7812 1600
Helpline: 020 7242 1010
www.tht.org.uk

HIV and AIDS charity for life: support, information and guidance. 'Buddy' support system.

United Kingdom Council for Psychotherapy
2nd floor
Edward House
2 Wakling Street
London EC1V 7LT
020 7014 9955
www.psychotherapy.org.uk

Regulatory body promoting practice, research, education and training in psychotherapy.

West Midlands SOBS
3 St Nicholas Close
Austrey
Atherstone
Warwickshire CV9 3EQ
Helpine: 01827 830679

Booklets available: *You Are Not Alone; Why, Why, Why Suicide;* and *Supporting Those Bereaved by Suicide.*

Winston's Wish
Head Office
Westoreland House
80–86 Bath Road
Cheltenham
Gloucester GL53 7JT
01242 515157
Helpline: 08452 030405
www.winstonswish.org.uk

Support for bereaved children and families. Information for schools and professionals as well as parents and carers.

Index

abuse 77, 78, 88, 102–3, 106
achievements 33, 94, 95, 96–7, 104, 105, 106, 184
adult children 77–8, 78–80, 83, 122, 137
advice 23–4, 32, 49
alcohol abuse 77, 78, 131–2
aloneness 71–2, 74
anger 39, 45, 48, 51, 71
  keeping angry strategy 129–30
  relationships 71, 72, 75, 80
animals 111
Attig, Thomas 15, 95, 109, 114, 182, 184
audio visual recordings 60, 105

Bad Day, Good Day exercise 142
Bayliss, Jean 52

beliefs 21, 24, 94, 103, 113, 116, 129, 164, 171, 172
bereavement 20
  basic philosophies 20–5
  basic practicalities 25–31
bereavement models 11, 33, 182
  Dual Process Model 133–4, 144–5
  Meaning Reconstruction 14
  Walter, Tony 35–6
bereavement theories 11, 12, 14, 17, 18, 33, 136, 182
  counsellors 164
  Freud, Sigmund 21, 65–6
  Romanoff, Bronna D. 37
Bible 108
biographies 60–1
Blob Tree 122, 140–1
boundaries 31, 172, 175
  time boundaries 25–6

Bowman, Ted 183
buttons 86–7, 142–3

carers 67, 76
children 17, 57, 58, 59, 121, 122
  bereaved young adults 77–8
  child's death 48, 70, 78–80
  child's suicide 12–13
  children as carers 67
churches 12, 18, 28, 29–30, 132, 171, 175, 177, 181
Cinderella Syndrome 125
clients 17, 24–5
  relationships 87–92
  stories 62–3
  suicidal thoughts 164, 176–80
  touch 27
  trust 44
collage 58, 61, 161
colleagues 13–14, 25, 28, 33, 55, 57, 82, 91, 93

confidentiality 28–9, 31, 178, 181
contracting 28–9
conversation 14, 15, 16, 18, 19
coping strategies 15, 16, 33, 119–22, 145
boxing up strategy 128–9
fund raising strategy 124
getting fit strategy 123–4
holding on to belongings strategy 127–8
humour strategy 133
impact on you as listener 143–5
isolation and withdrawal strategy 125–7
keeping angry strategy 129–30
keeping busy strategy 123
keeping life the same strategy 130–1
maintaining contact strategy 128
protective strategy 122–3
self-destructive strategy 131–2
self-help strategy 132–3
taking care of others strategy 124–5
victim strategy 131
what do you do with the strategy for coping? 135–9
what questions can you ask? 139–40
what techniques can you use? 140–3
counselling 11, 14, 16, 24
counsellors 12, 17, 24, 28, 37, 45, 77, 89, 164, 177, 180
Crabb, Larry 64
creative work 16, 17, 61, 86, 161
crying 23, 26–7, 44, 65, 120, 122, 136, 142
cultural issues 18, 90, 125, 147, 164, 171–2, 176

death 12–14, 15, 17, 20, 21, 144
accidental death 60, 66, 67, 76, 111
child's death 48, 70, 78–80
dying process 47–8
father's death 45–6, 57, 75, 95, 96
husband's death 53–4, 73–4, 109–10, 126
mother's death 13–14, 30, 46–7, 51–2, 74, 119–20
parent's death 69–70, 74–8

partner's death 50–1, 70, 71–4, 98–9
sibling's death 80–1
sudden death 12, 39, 43, 44, 47, 60, 71, 123, 149, 184
tragic death 44, 66, 122–3, 184
wife's death 39–40, 68, 136–7
dementia 13, 76
denial 47, 51, 60, 62, 71–2, 130–1, 148
despair 149, 150, 183
detachment 21, 65–6
diagnosis 39, 40, 42, 47
doctors 29, 38, 68, 76, 129, 131, 149, 178
Doka, Kenneth 15, 120, 134, 144
dreams 24, 59–60
creative expression 86
visits from the dead 149–50, 173–5
drug abuse 77, 78
Dual Process Model 133–4, 144–5

eating disorders 131
elements 16, 17, 18, 20, 31, 32–4
overview 186–8
embarrassment 13, 26, 107, 165–6, 170
emotions 23, 26, 43–4
emotional legacies 112
experts 23, 28, 32, 37, 63

families 15, 23, 28, 35
    coping strategies 122,
        124, 125–7, 130,
        133, 137, 140
    family feuds 48–9
    family tree 84–6
    journey of grief 154
    memory books 58–9
    relationships 65, 66,
        70, 71, 73, 81–2
    stories 39, 41, 45–6,
        56
father's death 45–6, 57,
    75, 95, 96
fitness 123–4, 137
Freud, Sigmund 21, 65–6
friends 13–14, 15, 16,
    17, 107
    relationships 65, 66
    touch 27
    working agreements 28
fund raising 124, 145

gardens 110, 111–12,
    123, 151
gender 15, 120, 144
grief 11, 15, 16, 18, 20,
    21, 97
    breaking bonds 65–6
    celebration of life 94–5
    coping strategies 133,
        134–5
    normal reactions 135
    stories 47
    young adults 77
grieving patterns 15,
    120–1, 125, 134,
    136–8, 140, 144
    blended 120

instrumental 120, 121,
    123, 124, 125,
    138, 140
    intuitive 120, 122,
        125, 137
guilt 12, 39, 48, 51, 149
    relationships 71, 72,
        75, 80, 81

healing 22–3, 37
health workers 12, 17,
    18, 28, 60
holidays 110–11
honesty 63, 71–2, 88,
    90, 92, 105–6, 157,
    158, 166, 175, 176,
    183
hospices 11, 15, 18, 26,
    47, 124, 179, 181
    children's hospices 110
hospitals 25, 26, 38, 39,
    40, 48, 68, 76, 78,
    80, 96, 129
house projects 110, 123,
    151
humour 133
husband's death 53–4,
    73–4, 109–10, 126

illness 38–9, 55, 97, 123,
    149
    relationships 66, 67–9,
        71–2, 76, 78, 79
intimacy 51, 69, 71, 165,
    167–70
isolation 125–7

jealousy 68–9, 75
journaling 59–60, 86
journey of grief 15, 16,
    33, 49, 146–7
    drawing or writing 161
    impact on you as
        listener 161–3
    phases 148–9, 149–50,
        150–1
    supervision 155–6
    tasks 148, 149, 150,
        151–2
    the long and winding
        road 153–4
    the railway track 154
    the river 153
    the rollercoaster 152–3
    the whirlpool 155
    tidal ebb and flow
        154–5
    what do you do with
        the journey?
        156–9
    what questions can you
        ask? 160
    what techniques can
        you use? 160–1

Klass, D. 21

learning disabilities 17
legacies 15, 16, 18, 33,
    107–14
    collections 113–14,
        127
    emotional legacies 112
    impact on you as
        listener 117–18

what do you do with the legacy? 114–15
what questions can you ask? 115–16
what techniques can you use? 116–17
letter writing 59, 60, 86
letting go 21, 22, 91, 127
breaking bonds 65–6, 75, 91, 127
life 12, 14, 15, 16, 21, 22, 33, 93–7
how do you celebrate the life? 97–103
impact on you as listener 105–6
successful lives 99–100
what questions can you ask? 103–4
what techniques can you use? 104–5
life lines 60–1, 160–1
life story books 57, 58–9, 61–2
listening 14, 15, 16, 17, 25
celebration of life 105–6
coping strategies 143–5
journey of grief 161–3
legacies 117–18
relationships 81–2, 87–92
stories 49–50, 62–3
suicidal thoughts 180–1

literary activities 86
loneliness 24, 66, 125–6, 127, 144, 150, 177
looking after oneself 30–1
loss 13, 14, 22, 31, 103, 148, 149, 183
coping strategies 121–2, 127, 133–4, 144–5
legacies 110, 111, 115
life line 160
relationships 73

marriage 45, 68, 75, 80, 83, 84, 101–2
Marshall, S. 45
Martin, Terry 15, 120, 134, 144
martyrs 125
Meaning Reconstruction Therapy 14, 37
medical mistakes 39, 48
medication 47, 68
memories 22, 46, 47, 54, 103
moving house 151
relationships 65, 66–7, 69–70
memory books 57, 58–9
memory boxes 57, 59
memory jars 57–8, 105
memory stones 57
mental health issues 177, 183
metaphors 152–5, 158–9, 160, 161–2
mothers 122

mother's death 13–14, 30, 46–7, 51–2, 74, 119–20
mourning 22, 73, 94, 120, 148–51, 162, 171
moving on 22, 34, 65, 129, 151

Narrative Therapy 36–7
Neimeyer, Robert 14, 15, 37–8, 94, 95, 108, 109, 116, 182
Nickman, S.L. 21
nightmares 24, 48, 59
notes 30–1, 89
nursing staff 11, 12, 39, 47, 68–9, 76, 82, 161, 177

pain 12, 14, 18, 21, 22–3, 31, 49, 97, 182, 183, 184
coping strategies 137
crying 136
journey of grief 149
relationships 67, 69, 75
palliative care 15, 18, 22, 52, 60
parents 67, 83
parent's death 69–70, 74–8
Parkes, Colin Murray 15, 147, 148–9, 149–50, 150–1, 162
partners 80, 83

partners *cont.*
  partner's death 50–1,
    70, 71–4, 98–9
  partners as carers 67
pastoral care 17, 18, 91,
    161
personality change 47–8,
    68
photographs 56–7, 86,
    105
poems 59, 86, 175
prayers 86
presence of the dead
    149–50, 173–5
professionals 14, 17, 18,
    22, 23, 25, 28, 32,
    89, 91, 124, 183
  health professionals 60,
    68
psychologists 12, 14, 15,
    37–8, 64, 147–8

questions
  celebration of life
    103–4
  coping strategies
    139–40
  journey of grief 160
  legacies 115–16
  relationships 82–4
  stories 54–5

reflection 50–2, 170, 172
regret 48, 50–1, 69, 72,
    73, 79, 91
relationships 15, 16, 33,
    64–71, 182

abusive relationships
    102–3
breaking bonds 65–6,
    75, 91, 127
death of a parent as an
    adult 74–8
death of an adult child
    78–80
death of partner or
    spouse 71–4
impact on you as
    listener 87–92
keeping angry strategy
    130
what do you do with
    the relationship?
    81–2
what questions can you
    ask? 82–4
what techniques can
    you use? 84–7
relief 76, 123, 127, 136,
    149, 152, 171
religion 18, 129, 171–2,
    176
rescue 90–1, 143, 183
Romanoff, Bronna D. 37

Schut, H. 133–4, 144
self harm 29, 77, 164,
    176–80
self help 132–3
sexuality 71, 164,
    165–70, 171, 176
siblings 75
  sibling's death 80–1
Silverman, P.R. 21
social workers 18

sorrow 21, 31, 49, 69,
    115, 127, 135, 182,
    184
  chronic sorrow 183
spiritualism 128, 175
spirituality 62, 113, 164,
    171–6
stones 57, 86–7, 142–3
stories 15, 16, 21, 32, 64,
    97–8
  bereavement work
    35–8
  components of a story
    42–5
  facts and feelings 50,
    63
  final chapter 46–9
  first story 38–40
  how many stories?
    40–2
  impact on you as
    listener 62–3
  middle stories 45–6
  what do you do with it?
    49–54
  what questions can you
    ask? 54–5
  what techniques can
    you use? 55–62
Stroebe, M. 65, 66
suicidal thoughts 164,
    176–80
  impact on you as
    listener 180–1
suicide 12–13, 29, 149
  coping strategies
    122–3
  relationships 71
  stories 44–5
  summarizing 52–4

supervision 18, 28–9, 29–30, 31, 182
  coping strategies 131, 132, 143
  inappropriate behaviour 166
  relationships 87–8, 88–9, 90, 92
  stories 45, 59, 63
  suicidal thoughts 180–1
support 11, 14, 17–18, 19, 31
  difficult issues 164–5
  looking after yourself 30–1
  supervision 29–30
  tears 26–7
  time 25–6
  working agreements 28–9

Taylor, Sally Flatteau 164
tears 26–7, 31, 136, 151
techniques 55–6, 63, 182–3
  audio-visual recordings 60, 105
  Bad Day, Good Day exercise 142
  biographical stories 60–61
  Blob Tree 122, 140–1
  buttons and stones 86–7, 142–3
  family tree 84–6
  journaling 59–60, 86
  journey of grief 160–1
  letter writing 59, 60, 86
  memory books 57, 58–9
  memory boxes 57, 59
  memory jars 57–8, 105
  photographs 56–7, 86, 105
  three memory stones 57
time 25–6
tissues 26
titles 25
tools see techniques
touch 26, 27, 31
treatment 42, 60, 68, 80, 101
trust 44, 45, 76

victims 103, 131, 143, 145
violence 88
voluntary workers 11, 12, 14, 17, 18, 20, 23–4, 32

Walter, Tony 15, 35–6, 43
wife's death 39–40, 68, 136–7
withdrawal 125–7
Worden, William 15, 22, 147, 148, 149, 150, 151–2, 162
working agreements 28–9